terra incognita

Terra Incognita as a series seeks to open a "thinking space" between the abandonment of politics often associated with postmodernism and the unreconstructed faith in politics which has characterized many modern emancipatory projects. Both of these positions function as grand narratives which circumscribe both theoretical and practical possibilities. In doing so, they have discouraged the thinking through of uncertainty.

Encompassing a range of theoretical and disciplinary approaches, the studies in *Terra Incognita* attempt to disrupt this opposition, expressing resistance, not only to 'grand narratives', but to any abstractions or conceptual frames which enact closure. The series probes how Western societies reconfigure themselves in currents flowing within and beyond their borders. Of particular interest are the theatres of struggle involving relationships with indigenous peoples, equality-seeking movements and state-fragmenting nationalist movements.

We are Not You

First Nations and Canadian Modernity

We are Not You

First Nations and Canadian Modernity

CLAUDE DENIS

broadview press

CANADIAN CATALOGUING IN PUBLICATION DATA

Denis, Claude, 1960–
     We are not you : First Nations and Canadian modernity

(Terra incognita)
Includes bibliographical references and index.
ISBN 1-55111-118-7

1.   Thomas, David – Trials, litigation, etc.
2.   Indians of North America – Legal status, laws, etc. – Canada.
3.   Indians of North America – Canada – Politics and government.

I.   Title.
II. Series: Terra incognita (Peterborough, Ont.).

KE7709.D46 1997   342.71 0872   C97-931604-9
KF8205.D46 1997

BROADVIEW PRESS
Post Office Box 1243, Peterborough, Ontario, Canada K9J 7H5

In the United States of America:
3576 California Road, Orchard Park, NY 14127

In the United Kingdom:
B.R.A.D. Book Representation & Distribution Ltd.,
244A, London Road, Hadleigh, Essex SS7 2DE

Broadview Press gratefully acknowledges the support of the Canada Council, the Ontario Arts Council, and the Ministry of Canadian Heritage.

This book was designed and readied for the press by Zack Taylor, Black Eye Design.

Printed in Canada

10 9 8 7 6 5 4 3 2 1

À ma mère, Hélène, et en mémoire
de ses soeurs, mes tantes Mariette et Suzanne.

Contents

Acknowledgements

← ── →

Danyèle Lacombe, Barbara Marshall, and David Schneiderman read through various versions of the whole manuscript and provided invaluable commentary and suggestions. At least as importantly, Barb, my friend and partner in editing *Terra Incognita*, has provided constant encouragement; David, excellent friend, reader, and purveyor of legal information, has made a uniquely rich contribution. Michael Harrison and Don LePan at Broadview have made the process of publishing the book a simple and pleasant one.

Now, where I should have begun: special thanks to Danyèle for believing in my work to the point of bearing the brunt of my 1995-1996 sabbatical leave, much of which I spent away from home.

This book had been in slow development for three years when I obtained the sabbatical leave from Faculté Saint-Jean, University of Alberta, allowing me to write most of the manuscript. Over this time, I benefited from the help and good will of many people in Edmonton, Montreal, Vancouver, and Victoria. I especially want to thank Paul Bernard, Bill Carroll, Jill Hightower, Dan Koenig, Veronica Strong-Boag, Rennie Warburton, and Margot Young – sorry Margot, but you know about alphabetical order. Ann at the University of Victoria's Women's Centre helped me track down some important information, as did people in the following institutions: the British Columbia Court Registry and Sheriff's Office, the Federal Crown Prosecutor's Office for BC, and the Royal Canadian Mounted Police. The comments of many people at conferences in Vancouver, Seattle, and Hermosillo (Mex.) have found their way in subsequent versions of my analysis. I also thank a member of a Vancouver Island First Nation who will only make a few appearances in these pages; but, as a result of two brief meetings, he put his mark on the whole book. I wish I could have learned more from him.

Some material in this book was previously published in the *International Journal of Canadian Studies* (Dec. 1996); and snippets on how "politics" means come from "Politics and Society" (co-authored with Trevor Harrison), in William Meloff and David Pierce (eds.) *An Introduction to Sociology*, (Scarborough (On.): Nelson Canada, 1994), 146-167.

Joseph Peters, in the
court of public opinion

Zen is saying, as Wittgenstein
said: 'Don't think: Look!'
– THOMAS MERTON[1]

L'Annonciation is a small town north-west of Montreal, in the Laurentians. Police there issued a press release one day in October 1995: arrests had been made in the kidnapping and beating of a man who had "disturbed" (burned, stolen from?) a marijuana field. Evidently, the people growing the marijuana had caught the man, taken him to their house, and punished him for tampering with their crop. He then escaped and called the police.[2]

Seven, almost eight years before, in March 1988, on Vancouver Island, another man was grabbed by several people just as he was getting out of the shower; he was taken to an isolated, empty building, and was beaten and given no food over the course of four days. He, Joseph Peters, was finally allowed to leave; he spent a night in hospital, spoke with the police, and eventually launched a lawsuit against his captors for "assault, battery, and false imprisonment." He did not, however, file an official complaint with the police, and no criminal charges were laid. In February 1992, four years after the event, he won his lawsuit. That is when I first heard of the misadventure of Joseph Peters, when *The Globe and Mail* ran an article reporting on the British Columbia Supreme Court's decision, quickly followed by an editorial. Soon after, I had the first inkling of building a book around this, the *Peters v. Campbell* case.

● ● ●

Time and space are not what set the two events, in the Laurentians and on Vancouver Island, apart from one another. Nor is the difference in police

---

1   Merton, in Wu (1996: 13). Wittgenstein writes "don't think, but look!" at paragraph 66 of *Philosophical Investigations* (3rd edition, 1968). In later references to Wittgenstein's work, the symbol § will be used to indicate a paragraph number.

2   From a CBC-Radio news report in Montreal, 10h00, 18 October 1995; and *La Presse*, 19 October 1995.

intervention of great importance, in and of itself. What, then? – because there *is* a profound difference between the two cases.

When the BC Supreme Court convened to hear Joseph Peters' complaint against Frank Campbell and six co-defendants, the seven men agreed that they had "grabbed" Peters, held him for four days without food, and subjected him to the various treatments he described. But, they strenuously argued, they had not assaulted, battered, or falsely imprisoned him: they had, rather, put him through the ritual initiation to their people's traditional practice of "syewen,"[3] typically called "spirit dancing" by outsiders,[4] their people being the Coast Salish indigenous people of British Columbia and Washington state. The defendants further claimed that the Canadian Constitution protected and affirmed their right to carry out such rituals: this is where their story acquires an emblematic importance. They were asking, in other words, that the lawsuit be dismissed on the grounds that the event claimed by the plaintiff Joseph Peters – "assault, battery, and false imprisonment" – had never actually happened. What had happened, instead, was a constitutionally protected religious ceremony – and that was none of the BC Supreme Court's business.

The article in *The Globe and Mail* described syewen as "involving fasting and confinement until an individual hears 'the song of his guardian spirit,' which leads to the initiate dancing and singing a song." This is accurate as far as it goes, but only insofar as *the initiation* to syewen is concerned. This is an important distinction, to which we will return. It should also be added that the fasting and confinement normally last four days and aim at producing an ecstatic trance out of which the dance and song arise, connecting the dancer with her or his guardian spirit. Once the initiation is completed, a process begins that may last as long as four years, in which the new dancer learns with the help of fellow dancers to live harmoniously with her or his spirit. The continuing relationship struck between individual and guardian spirit is then marked at annual "Winter Dances," large-scale ceremonial events involving much of the community (see Suttles, 1987).

The presiding judge eventually ruled against Peters's initiators, but only after considering whether or not the Canadian Constitution actually did rec-

---

3 This spelling of "syewen" is an adaptation from Suttles (1987), for the sake of retaining a standard English alphabet. Amoss (1978) has a different orthography, further from English. Still, even simplified in this way, "syewen" retains great resemblance to the spoken word as I have heard it from members of the Longhouse, the practitioners of syewen. In these pages, I will follow the usage of the Longhouse, and speak of syewen, not spirit dancing, except of course when quoting from a variety of outsiders.

4 The practice of naming is of crucial importance in society, whether one deals with names of individuals or of collectivities, of things or people; and it will play a central part in this book. On naming and the relationship between aboriginal peoples and the European tradition, see Derrida (1967: 157–173), Owens (1992: 284–297), Todorov (1992); and for a multifaceted look at the naming of the "Indian," see Gómez-Moriana and Trottier (1993).

ognize their right to initiate someone without her or his consent. He agreed that the initiators had good intentions, and that they had wanted to help Joseph Peters; but if Peters did not want to be helped, they had no right to coerce him into an initiation. The marijuana growers of L'Annonciation, for their part, had no legal instruments at their disposal which might have redefined their agricultural activities, kidnapping, and beating, as something entirely legal, much less constitutionally protected. And they were not functioning in a cultural context in which these activities would have been understood as non-deviant: their own cultural context defined their activities as illegal. But by denying the aboriginal right, the Canadian state – through the British Columbia Supreme Court – ended up treating both cases as violating the same central rule of *modern* societies: the state's claim to a monopoly on legitimate violence. In "Western" countries, this is a claim enforced when necessary by police and the courts, but more often by consent of the great majority of "law abiding citizens" (for it is when citizens consent to abide by the law that, *ipso facto*, the state's monopoly of legitimate violence is enforced).

This is the first issue at the heart of this book: the denial of a claimed aboriginal right by the Canadian state – its sources, its logic, and its impact on the relations in Canada between *whitestream*[5] society and First Nations.[6] A key element of how this issue will be addressed here is how the relationship is constructed and disseminated in discourse through the media, thereby contributing to the fabrication of national (and other) identities for both whitestream Canadians and members of indigenous peoples. One of the aims of this book, then, is to undermine readings of Canada vs First Nations that construct the relationship in antagonistic terms of us vs them, civilized vs barbarian, modern vs traditional, individual rights vs collective rights – readings that, in so doing, obscure the role that relations between women and men play in social life.

This brings me to the book's second fundamental aim, which is to put modernity itself into question. That is to say, there may be something to be learned from a case like this, *from the aboriginal side of this case*, about moder-

---

5   Adapting from feminism's notion of "malestream," I say whitestream to indicate that Canadian society, while principally structured on the basis of the European, "white," experience, is far from being simply "white" in socio-demographic, economic, and cultural terms. Within feminist scholarship, "malestream" was initially Mary O'Brien's (1981) concept and later gained wide circulation.

6   I use this term in a generic sense synonymous with such other terms as "aboriginal people," "native people," "indigenous people" – all of which appear in these pages. This usage of "First Nation" is different from common political parlance in Canada that restricts the term to "Indian" bands as defined and organized by the *Indian Act*, to the exclusion of Inuit and Metis peoples and non-status Indians. I am ignoring these legally derived distinctions precisely to highlight the source of the legitimacy of aboriginal claims: they are peoples, or nations, and they were first to occupy this land of the Americas.

nity's own limitations and shortcomings. Beyond the specifics of the *Peters v. Campbell* story, this agenda is driven by the theoretical outlook usually labelled "poststructuralism,"[7] whose tendency to put modernity in the hot seat is a notorious marker. Thus, poststructuralism is critical of modernity's claim that society's political self-making can and will bring about fundamental human emancipation. This ambition is specifically modern in that it removes God, or more generally the spiritual, from the centre of human life and replaces it with society, with "Man";[8] and it is political in the sense that purposive collective action – the transformative work of society upon itself – is given the mandate to bring about human emancipation.

When Frank Campbell and the other initiators took it upon themselves to "help" Joseph Peters (we will see later why they thought he needed help), they did not put their hope in socio-political resources and solutions: they situated his need and their own action in the spiritual realm – and they did this not in the privacy of their own individual lives, but as public-minded members of a community. This is consistent with what the Report of the Royal Commission on Aboriginal Peoples writes of the aboriginal world:

> The fundamental feature of Aboriginal world view was, and continues to be, that all of life is a manifestation of spiritual reality. We come from spirit; we live and move surrounded by spirit; and when we leave this life we return to a spirit world. All perceptions are conditioned by spiritual forces, and all actions have repercussions in spiritual reality. (Canada, 1996A: 628)[9]

There are challenges addressed to modernity in such an outlook, in the actions of Joseph Peters's initiators, and in the experience sought in syewen itself – and this is happening right here and now, not in some distant exotic land or many centuries ago. In this sense, as John Milbank has noted, to the

---

7 It has become customary at this point of an Introduction to launch into a discussion of how "poststructuralism" relates to "postmodernism", involving an earnest awareness of the multiple senses of the latter term. For a useful take on the exegesis of "postmodern", see Turner (1990a). I am loath to do it myself, beyond remarking that I am speaking of poststructuralism with a specific view to its theoretical outlook on language. As Chris Weedon (1987: 22) has noted, "(i)ts founding insight, taken from the structural linguistics of Ferdinand de Saussure, is that language, far from reflecting an already given social reality, constitutes social reality for us. Neither social reality nor the 'natural' world has fixed intrinsic meanings which language reflects or expresses." More on this outlook below.

8 On this modern ambition, see Touraine (1992).

9 When the Royal Commission issued its Report at the end of 1996, this book was very far advanced. I have been unable, as a result, to take full account of the Report. But I have had time to draw on some of it; in particular, Volume 1, Part 3 and Volume 2, Part 1, Chapter 3 offer perspectives that are highly relevant to the analysis presented here. In the chapters to come, I will make reference to some of these.

considerable extent that modernity can be understood as a critique of religion, one might expect critics of modernity to take issue with that critique.

More widely still, there is a link in the challenge presented to modernity by poststructuralism and syewen on the one hand, and Eastern philosophical traditions – I am thinking in particular of Zen Buddhism – on the other. Far from bringing it forward arbitrarily (in the sense that the analysis could well proceed without it), I am suggesting that this link pulls together the theoretical and experiential / spiritual strands of the challenge: Zen articulates a spiritual experience[10] that has a strong "family resemblance"[11] with syewen, in a way that is remarkably consistent with poststructuralist theory. Thus, what Michel Foucault called "the limit-experience"[12] is a kind of experience often attained through severe bodily exertion or discipline (whether starving, infliction of pain, exercised breathing, etc.), beyond linguistic expression, one variant of which is generally referred to as *mysticism*. This is why Andrew Wernick has been able to write of "the Buddhist conception of (not-)self which can be detected in the work of Foucault and others" (1992: 57).

This second concern of the book, it turns out, shapes the first, both in its direction and its limitations – its political pitch, I might say in a direct appropriation of Stanley Cavell's (1994) transfer of the term "pitch" from music to philosophy. In this sense, this book's project is that of a radical critique of the relationship between First Nations and Canadian society. The critique is radical not in the sense of being somehow politically extreme, but because of its position that while political oppression is an undeniable reality, there is no such thing as human liberation through politics. Social power, in short, is not abolished among the Indians. Someone interested in ultimate liberation, then, ought to look past the political, somewhere other than in modernity's faith in "Man".

Stated as baldly as this, the argument may seem overdone, modernity's Man rather made of straw. One reason, of course, is that sophisticated moderns are not, nowadays, likely to use the word "ultimate" all that often[13]: too many high humanist hopes have been ruthlessly crushed by the appalling twentieth century. (Not that everything has been appalling; but the century's horrors are sufficiently large and perverse, it seems to me, that

---

10 As we will see below, there is something paradoxical in saying that Zen *articulates* this experience; this is a paradox which I inherit from expository writings on Zen.

11 This is a phrase favoured by Wittgenstein (1968: § 67), to refer to "a complicated network of similarities overlapping and criss-crossing: sometimes overall similarities, sometimes similarities of detail" (§ 66). On Wittgenstein's notion of family resemblance, see Fogelin (1996).

12 On the centrality of the limit-experience to Foucault's outlook, see Miller (1993).

13 Although one *will* find the phrase "ultimate reality" in John Milbank's (1992) discussion of Heidegger and the postmodern agenda on religion.

"appalling" should qualify as one of its chief adjectives.) Still, we "progressives" should ask ourselves to what extent we have shed not only our predecessors' candid phrases but also the basic optimist creed that nourished their words, and that ought, at the very least, to be re-examined and scaled down. Again: how thoughtful is it to carry on, at the end of the twentieth century, with a humanist optimism that began to strain with, say, World War I?

Such are the two streams of concerns, interrelated but distinct, that have made this book come together. First, the urgency of undermining the racism and sexism of Canadian society, so as to help the development of what I call *aboriginality* (i.e. the cultural project of aboriginal peoples),[14] one important component of which is self-government . To borrow again from Cavell, it is "an emergency that neutralizes prudence" (Cavell, 1994: ix): the emergency of what it is important to say in Canada today, against the political and professional prudence which would lead one to follow the advice of Voltaire's Candide, that "we must cultivate our garden" (Voltaire, 1963 [1759]: 299).

In the context of this book, political imprudence is motivated by the need to foster conditions that will allow First Nations to exercise their sovereignty – what in political debate is often called their inherent right to self-government – with the support of Canadians. More broadly, it has to do with the fostering of a more democratic Canada, a Canada that stops silencing women and that frees itself from its colonialist discursive matrix, so that it can reinvent itself and respect not only the sovereignty of indigenous peoples, but also the nationhood of *my* people, the people of Quebec: indeed, this is where my own garden may be seen to share at least some ground with others'.

As for the professional corner of the garden, imprudence involves my venturing well outside the bounds of what might be considered my specialties. I certainly claim no great expertise in either aboriginal spirituality or Zen Buddhism, but I do think that engaging them seriously is my only hope of hitting my analytical and socio-political targets. There may well be nothing original in my plowing of one or the other corner of the garden, but it is in making the unlikely connections that, perhaps, imprudence can bear fruit. As Peter Gay asked of *Candide*'s last sentence, "precisely how big is the garden we are enjoined to cultivate? We are told to cultivate *our* garden, but how much in this world is ours?" (Gay, in Voltaire, 1963: xxi. Emphasis in original).

---

14 The word *aboriginality* can be found in the anthropological literature, to design a state of things among aboriginal peoples before the encounter with European societies. In that sense, it is a static notion, belonging wholly to the past. I use it in a dynamic and contemporary manner, to designate a cultural project, of the same order as modernity.

• • •

Before we proceed with the analysis of *Peters v. Campbell*, a few words are in order about the intellectual pitch of the book. One hope is that graduate students and professors will find that the book makes a contribution to the critique of modernity in general, and of Canadian modernity in particular. As importantly, I have written it hoping that senior undergraduate students and others with no experience of graduate school may read it with profit, if perhaps also with some difficulty. The latter stems from my determination to address the story of Joseph Peters's community in all its complexity, especially in its interpellation of issues at the heart of current theoretical debates in the social sciences and humanities. I am fairly confident of having succeeded in my attempt to make the book accessible, with the possible exception of Chapter 7, much (but not all) of which is concerned with a philosophical discussion that seemed to resist my attempts at accessible writing. I do not think, however, that the difficulty of that chapter stems entirely from the topic itself. Rather, it seems to me that unfamiliarity is the largest source of difficulty, and the best antidote for that is to get acquainted with this foreign (and therefore difficult) material.

I have not wanted to foreground theoretical issues in (most of) the text, in the sense that it is the reading of *Peters v. Campbell* that drives the analysis. But the fundamental wager of the book is that from this particular story we should learn general things about modernity and Canada of course, but also about nationalism, colonialism, human rights, gender relations, and so on. It is in this spirit that I have kept the chapter headings to their simplest expression: one concept at the head of each chapter, highlighting one (but not the only) central conceptual dimension of that chapter. Not that the titles are self-explanatory: the very specificities of the story and of my positioning in telling it, ensure that the relevance of concepts such as colonialism and gender takes many unexpected twists and turns. Also because of this, I cannot hope to provide a chapter summary here that would do justice to those meanderings. There is a tension between headings and text, that may in fact be seen as a resource for reading, an invitation to trouble the ostensible stability of the written words.

Chapter 1
Nationalisms

◄──►

What is a whitestream Canadian to make of the misadventures of Joseph Peters, as told by *The Globe and Mail*? The initial news report is written in such a way that the whitestream reader is very likely to find what was done to Joseph Peters outrageous. In looking at Peters, his initiators, and the Court, such a reader will probably think that a forced initiation to syewen is barbarian and savage, and that the Court's upholding of individual rights against tribal collective rights is the civilized thing to do. This point is further driven home in an editorial a few days after the first article, warning Canadians against jumping too quickly on the aboriginal self-government bandwagon because there are serious issues of right and wrong to be considered. Left to themselves, in other words, natives cannot necessarily be trusted to do what "we" know to be the right things.

Many readers having seen too many popular western movies with their scenes of "Indian" torture,[1] the Peters story as told in *The Globe and Mail* will easily find its place in the pattern, reinforcing it in the process. The reader, in short, is likely to be comforted in his or her modern, civilized, liberal identity, and in disapproval of pre-modern barbaric tribalism. In Canada as elsewhere, such readings of the whitestream vs "Indian" relationship are dominant, hegemonic, notwithstanding an English-Canadian public opinion that has appeared increasingly sympathetic to "them" since the mid-1980s. It is, for example, to this kind of dominant outlook that the *1991* Delgamuukw judgement belongs.[2] In this important decision, Chief Justice Allan McEachern of the BC Supreme Court could write that the Gitksan and Wet'suwet'en peoples barely constituted a human society prior to the establishment of a British colony on the west coast:

---

1 On culturally prevalent images of "the Indian" in North American culture, see Francis (1992).

2 At the same time that it is inscribed quite logically in the established legal tradition; much more on this below. See also Asch (1992). On the Delgamuukw decision, see also Cassidy (1992); Justice McEachern was eventually overturned on appeal.

I do not accept the ancestors (of the aboriginal plaintiffs) "on the ground" behaved as they did because of "institutions." Rather I find they more likely acted as they did because of survival instincts that varied from village to village. (McEachern, *Delgamuukw v. The Queen*, quoted in Asch, 1992: 225)

Needless to say, this kind of outlook on aboriginal peoples in general or on an event as specific as the *Peters v. Campbell* story, is not going to help Canadians appreciate and respect aboriginal claims to an "inherent right to self-government." This phrase, "inherent right to self-government," is the concept that has been favoured for many years by First Nations leadership, especially the Assembly of First Nations (AFN). It has entered Canada's standard political vocabulary during the constitutional negotiations of the mid-1980s, and was accepted by the country's premiers and prime minister in 1992's "Charlottetown round" of negotiations. The referendum defeat of the Charlottetown Accord, however, left First Nations without any gains in the constitutional game.[3]

The key word in the phrase is "inherent," in that it refers to the fact that First Nations occupied this land first and therefore were sovereign self-governing societies, and that they never gave up their sovereignty. It could be said, in this sense, that a label at once more evocative and more precise for this concept would be to speak of the First Nations' *sovereign right* to self-government.[4] This label would, however, invite a more radical political stance than what the AFN has actually advocated, closer to the positions of the Mohawk people and of the Alberta Treaty Chiefs: it suggests that aboriginal peoples might stand *outside* the Canadian constitution, in the kind of relationship with Canada regulated by international treaties.[5]

This, it seems to me, is what the logic of "inherent right" leads to; but this position goes beyond what most chiefs within the AFN have been willing to consider so far. A disjunction has thus developed between policy goals and discursive claims, leading perhaps to the kind of confusion upon which, according to writer Lee Maracle (1996), the aboriginal elite thrives through its access to government funds and recognition; whether or not this is at the expense of aboriginal people themselves, as Maracle argues, is not an easy thing to establish. As well, the post-Charlottetown period has not been kind to the political standing of aboriginal leaders and their claims, leading for

---

3   What such a gain would have actually accomplished remains uncertain. For a severe critique of the focus on this principle as the illusion of naive leaders, see Boldt (1993).

4   The concept of *inherent* right, however, has one element which *sovereign* right lacks: an explicit statement of the source of the right – the fact of first (sovereign) occupancy.

5   More on this later in this chapter, and in Chapter 4. On the extra political baggage carried by "sovereign," see Boldt (1993).

instance to AFN Grand Chief Ovide Mercredi's growing anger at the Canadian political leadership and to a radicalization of his outlook. At the 1996 AFN annual meeting, he advocated a turn towards a goal of "sovereignty-association" similar to what Quebec nationalists have been seeking. Reacting to Mercredi's argument, former AFN National Chief David Ahenakew commented: "We lack the guts to implement the things we say we want."[6]

In any case, First Nations are demanding that their "inherent right" be recognized, not given: they already have it, but whitestream Canada has  never recognized that this is the case. Lack of recognition would not be all that important, the argument goes, if embedded within it there were not an unequal power relation: the political ability to refuse to recognize is dependent upon that inequality, at the same time that it reproduces it. This is what makes Canada, still today, a colonialist society. The logic of the argument of "inherent right" is at the core of this book.[7] On the basis of the "inherent right" logic, both the *Delgamuukw v. The Queen* and the *Peters v. Campbell* judgements are radically wrong-headed.[8] They do maintain colonialism in Canada. And, upon reading about Joseph Peters's ordeal in *The Globe and Mail* that day in February 1992, this is what made me sit up: "I'm in favour of self-government," I thought, "but does that mean having to accept people being treated like this? I can't accept *this*!"

It is the contradiction between my acceptance of the self-government principle and my spontaneous revulsion at its particular application to Joseph Peters that pulled me into this story. I eventually found that there was more to it than what *The Globe and Mail* reported, not only in terms of understanding the cultural context in which Joseph Peters' initiators functioned, but also of uncovering a whole gendered dimension of the events – and that gendered dimension casts a very different light on Joseph Peters's story. Thus, it will also turn out that gender relations are a central and obscured element in all the stages of the *Peters v. Campbell* case: the initial events, the trial and judicial decision, and the telling of the story in the media.

I do not want to say too much about the gender nexus at this early point, because much of the drama in the *Peters v. Campbell* story turns on the fact

---

6   See Anne McIlroy, "Mercredi unveils last-ditch plan," *The Globe and Mail*, 9 July 1996, A1, A3.

7   Whether it is a good idea to build a political strategy on the basis of that right is another story: the fact that the word "inherent" is much less evocative than "sovereign" has surely helped in obtaining general support for inherent right, and in that sense it has surely served a useful purpose. But it is of little help in negotiating treaties such as the Nisga'a Accord (see below) in 1995-96, for governments can pay lip service to "inherent right" at the same time that they negotiate in a manner that belies that recognition. In this new context, the recognized right can be more useful to whitestream governments than to aboriginal peoples.

8   This is also the case for the more recent *Van der Peet* (1996) decision of the Supreme Court of Canada, which reaffirms the sovereignty of the Crown over aboriginal rights. For critiques of this decision, see Asch (1997) and several articles in *Constitutional Forum*, 8:2 (Winter), 1997.

that gender is *obscured*, as well as central, in the events and their narration by the media and the Court. This is why I have placed the full discussion of this nexus in the very middle of the book. But disclosing the key now, explaining what specific role gender relations played in the initiation of Joseph Peters, would betray the complexity of the situation. Part of the ambition of this book is to underline the difficulty of understanding, to show that the process of *getting* there matters perhaps as much as the fact of being there.

The articulation of the gender nexus in *Peters v. Campbell* is consistent with the trend in the politics of redefining the relationship between Canadian society and indigenous peoples. This process has become further complicated in recent years by the salience of gender issues, such as the question of whether aboriginal women would be helped by the application of the Canadian Charter of Rights and Freedoms to aboriginal self-government. There is nothing surprising in this salience, my feminist friends would argue, since gender relations are typically central and obscured in social life in general. This is not to say, however, that it is a simple or straightforward thing to articulate intercultural and gender processes. The analysis in the pages that follow bears directly on this question, including the vexed issue of Charter rights vs self-government. While confirming the issue's great difficulty, it will argue that only a consideration of concrete situations – as opposed to a high-minded faith in decontextualized principles – can actually clear up some of the confusion.

● ● ●

How much of this world is ours? Peter Gay's question about *Candide*, quoted in the Introduction, alludes to the book's second concern, of putting modernity into question. This is at once more personal and more general than the first goal, of destabilizing established Aboriginal / Canadian discursive relations. It has to do with a writer's mode of intervention in/upon the world and upon him- or herself. While the first concern is squarely sociopolitical (at least up to the point where it reaches the limits of the political), this one raises issues generally associated with philosophy and autobiography, with the works, in particular of Nietzsche, Thoreau, Wittgenstein, Foucault, and Cavell, and with a large part of both Taoism and Zen. Involved here is a willingness to change oneself so as (following Nietzsche and Foucault) to "become what one is," by putting into question the cognitive categories that constitute oneself. This must result in a greater opening to the other, a blurring and displacement of the self / other pre-existing boundaries, "a taking up of the world that is humanly a question of giving it up" (Cavell, 1994: 36) – evoking once again connections with "the void" pointed to by Zen Buddhism. John C.H. Wu writes:

... waking (to reality) is a strictly personal experience, as personal as eating and drinking. All external things are but a reflection of our "original face," and all external teachings are but an echo of the true music of our self-nature. Let no one identify himself with his mere reflection or echo; it is only by seeing one's self-nature that he becomes actually what he is in essence. (Wu, 1996: 58)[9]

It is probably useful at this point to introduce some elements of definition of mysticism, and to discuss issues of contemporary social theory that provide some of my basic guideposts. Indeed, the consideration of syewen as mystical limit-experience is one of the book's anchors, although the analysis of how modernity is challenged by this will have to wait until Chapter 7.

Defining mysticism is a notoriously difficult affair, as indicated by Thomas Merton's contradictory characterizations of the relationship between Christian and Zen mysticisms. Merton writes that "you can hardly set Christianity and Zen side by side and compare them. This would almost be like trying to compare mathematics and tennis" (Merton, in Wu, 1996: 1, 2). Foucault echoes Merton's warning, noting that Christian and Zen mysticisms are vastly different, the former being intensely involved with the self and the latter seeking to transcend it (Foucault, 1994A). But John Wu offers a sharp rebuttal to Foucault and this first Merton quotation in his summing up of a story relating the teachings of Ma-Tsu Tao-I: "Self-discovery ... is the real meaning of [Zen]" (1996: 75). Merton himself writes, only a few pages after the mathematics-and-tennis dismissal: "When we set Christianity and Buddhism side by side, we must try to find the points where a genuinely common ground between the two exists" (Merton, in Wu, 1996: 7). To which Roger Bastide, the French anthropologist of mysticism, offers a synthesis that, while having in mind Christian mystics, resembles what others say of Zen:

> (M)ysticism is a transformation of the personality, from which the self is emptied along with instincts and distinctive tendencies, in order as it were to get out of itself and commune with the object of its adoration. This lived experience can just as well be translated in intellectual terms: if all knowledge presupposes a relationship between subject and object, the knowing subject and the known object, mysticism will eliminate the first of these terms; the contemplating subject identifies fully and entirely with the thing contemplated. (Bastide, 1975: 13, 14. My translation)

---

9 Sensitive poststructuralists will cringe at words such as "reflection", "true", "self-nature", "essence". But it is important to look past the words that, in a Western context, we have learned to dislike: in the context of the Tao and of Zen, these words can be seen as expressing the distrust toward language which is a hallmark of the poststructuralist critique of the metaphysics of presence.

It would be easy to settle with Bastide's synthesis as a satisfactory common ground. But I would rather leave "mysticism" hovering somewhere in the space between the claims made for it by Bastide, Merton, Foucault, and Wu. This should act as a marker of the necessary elusiveness of the common ground between culturally distinct experiences that share the label. Michel de Certeau (1987) does something like that by refusing to assume a *thing* hiding behind the texts of a literary / spiritual tradition in sixteenth- and seventeenth-century Europe that adopted the label mysticism for itself. De Certeau's discourse analysis is content to delineate literary mysticism's constitution of "a new knowledge space," characterized by "[a] manner of practising received language *differently*" (de Certeau, 1987: 28, 29. My translation; emphasis in the original). Doing otherwise, doing more in seeking to name that assumed thing, de Certeau writes, would be to exorcise it, to "transform into a particular religious representation … the question that appears as the figure of *the limit*" (De Certeau, 1987: 27. My translation, and emphasis added.).

Limit-experience may amount to (for lack of a better word) ecstatic states, whether in the mystical tradition in Christianity, the "spirit quest" of western North America's indigenous peoples (of which syewen is a component), or Zen and its constitutive distrust of language.[10] For Zen, "words are inadequate to express the truth of ultimate reality" (Nhât Hanh, 1995: 41). Thus, "the practice of Zen is the hammer used to break the chains of illusion that binds us to the world of concepts" (Nhât Hanh, 1995: 44). Some of the theoretical link of Zen with contemporary Western philosophy, in fact, is expressed by Thomas Merton, in the quotation at the beginning of the Introduction. And Wittgenstein defined philosophy as "a battle against the bewitchment of our intelligence by means of language" (1968: § 109).

Coming after Wittgenstein, poststructuralist theory also distrusts language. This is one reason why language/discourse is made its chief object of interest: language does not transparently express ultimate reality, and we are fools to think it does. But language produces its own reality, which structures the social world: social reality is, in other words, essentially discursive. This theoretical agenda is indeed at work in Drucilla Cornell's reformulation of deconstruction as "the philosophy of the limit," stemming from that perspective's work of exposing "the quasi-transcendental conditions that establish any system … as a system"; this results, in Jacques Derrida's work, in "continually point[ing] to the failure of idealism to capture the real" (Cornell, 1992: 1). Hence the insistent association of Derrida's work with

---

10 This does not mean that language is not involved *in* the mystic's limit-experience: the "mystic fable" (de Certeau, 1987) among other narrations of the limit-experience would quickly give the lie to such a notion. It is also the case, however, that these narrations affirm their failure to communicate that experience. How language articulates an experience at the limit of language is intensely problematic – and beyond the scope of this book.

the tradition of negative theology which, "as practised by an Eckhart or a John of the Cross, is a prohibition against *any* thematizing of divine presence, any ultimate return to an analogy of being between God and the subject" (Rowan Williams, 1992: 72).[11] And, in a paraphrase of Judith Butler's work, Allison Weir writes that "all identity categories are expressions of the metaphysics of substance which is entrenched in language" (Weir, 1996: 6).

The gap between social/discursive reality and "ultimate reality" is the space in which the limit-experience dwells, silently. And so, as the limit-experience takes us out of language, it also takes us out of the social world into the domain of the uncommunicable, and of spirituality. This is what for many will be the unexpected meeting point of Zen and the concerns of Michel Foucault,[12] and more broadly of postmodern theory with theological concerns.[13] One might conclude, then, with only a hint of mischief, that the *teaching* of Zen is a way of *practising* poststructuralist theory. Thus, the stance common to poststructuralism and Zen that language is not to be trusted as an expression of reality, is encapsulated in the well-known Zen advice of master to student to "listen to the sound of one hand clapping." It is to be hoped that the student's puzzlement at what this may mean will eventually turn to a questioning of language itself and its relationship to ultimate reality.

●　●　●

The broad theoretical aspects of both concerns motivating the book, as well of course as those that bear directly on *Peters v. Campbell*, are dealt with at length in the book. Other aspects, that connect more to my personal situation and outlook, run between the lines: they will not be articulated explicitly again. It will be seen that what is involved is not merely personal, but rather a kind of fusion of the book's political and self-searching concerns. While every book is somehow about its author, writing that makes explicitly autobiographical moves carries its own kind of rhetorical complexities.[14]

---

11 After a career of refusing to address the claim / criticism that he was a practitioner of negative theology, Derrida finally admitted that at least some of his work is virtually indistinguishable from it. He admitted this, only to withdraw it in the subsequent typically (and, I would add, quite proper) deconstructive move. See Derrida (1987B). On spirituality in his work, see also Derrida (1987A).

12 Other than the fact that Zen is a form of limit-experience, which brings it of necessity into the ambit of his most fundamental quest (on this see Miller, 1993), Foucault has been at least tangentially interested in Zen. See Foucault (1994A) and the photograph of Foucault at a Japanese Zen monastery in 1978, reproduced in *Magazine littéraire*, 325, October 1994, p.55.

13 On this meeting point, see Berry and Wernick (1992).

14 On this issue, see Probyn (1993).

I write these lines barely a year after a referendum on the sovereignty of Quebec ended in a tie (50.6% "no", 49.4% "yes");[15] and when the tension between Quebec's national aspirations and Canada's obstinate and increasingly intolerant resistance to them is reaching a degree far above anything seen in my lifetime, including the 1970 "October Crisis" when the Front de libération du Québec kidnapped and killed a member of the Quebec government's cabinet.[16] As well, for the first time in the last two hundred years of often tense French / English cohabitation, indigenous peoples are playing an important part in the current difficulties, their claims to autonomy having become a weapon of choice in Canadian attempts to delegitimate the Québécois struggle. There are, here, two tragedies – and, in the face of greater suffering across the world, I use the word "tragedy" advisedly – precisely because Canada is one of the more peaceful, prosperous, and democratic countries on the planet.

To begin, we have to think of Canada as an unequal and conflictual partnership between three peoples: in order of dominance, the Canadian (by this I mean "Anglo-Canadian"), Québécois, and First Nation peoples. I want to note here that this sense of nationhood-in-conflict is not a natural fact, but a historically constructed one, with particular configurations of gender, class, and "race" relationships within the nation. As Stanley Fish (1995) writes in another context, however, it is not because something is historically constructed that it is not real or important, or that it does not engage people's (sometimes uneasy) loyalties and frame their practice. As well, if it is important to recognize the partiality of national identity in the context of the tense multiplicity of identity politics, there is no sense in calling for all-out political fragmentation as the remedy for the oppressive unity of something like nationhood (see Phillips, 1993). Canada, then, is a three-nation partnership, but this is, in fact, unacknowledged by the dominant anglo-Canadian partner.

The first tragedy is that, largely through intolerance born of being thoroughly possessed by their own national identity, Canadians are pushing Quebec toward an unnecessarily "hard" separation – a highly dangerous process, both in terms of socioeconomic costs for everyone concerned and in that it raises the possibility of violence (especially if the current Canadian fad of threatening to partition Quebec is not stopped very quickly),[17] something that would have been unthinkable until very recently. In this process, First Nations are allying themselves with the dominant against the middle

---

15 Of the roughly five million eligible voters, 93.5% exercised their right, and the "no" side obtained 52,000 more votes than the "yes" side did. See Monière et Côté (1995).

16 A British diplomat was also kidnapped, and later released unharmed. On the October crisis and the history of the FLQ, see Cardin (1990).

17 See Denis (1996).

partner, so that aboriginal claims are used against Quebec's claims. Indeed, over the last several years,[18] aboriginal claims have gained in legitimacy among Canadians in exact proportion to the loss of legitimacy of Quebec nationalism. It is clear, in this respect, that aboriginal claims are *used* by Canadians for their deleterious effect on Quebec. This raises very ominous prospects for the ability of First Nations to finally obtain autonomy, respect, and compensation for what they have been put through.

This is not to say that Québécois and First Nations claims to nationhood and autonomy would necessarily be easy to reconcile without the interference of Canadian strategies. Chances are that Quebec would in any case have difficulty shedding its own colonialist pretentions. But there is no reason in principle to think that, once the interference is bracketed, Quebec would be any more resistant to aboriginal claims than Canada has been and remains.

And this is the second tragedy: after they have been well used by Canadians in their campaign to crush Quebec nationalism, First Nations will be returned to neglect and injustice, forgotten once again and increasingly resented as they refuse to keep quiet. One may be doubtful, for instance, that if the initiation of Joseph Peters had happened ten years from now – when, one hopes, self-government will be a reality – a thoroughly aboriginal process would have had the mandate to address his complaint. My point is that both Québécois and First Nation claims against Canada ought to be recognized and affirmed *and* that First Nation claims against Quebec ought to be recognized and affirmed.

The First Nation / Canadian alliance against Quebec makes it unlikely that either set of claims will get anywhere without some kind of disaster for everyone involved. The present dynamic between Quebec and Canada, in which Canadians are playing increasingly hard ball, is leading indeed to a "hard" separation. And the frustration, anger, and despair of (especially) young aboriginal women and men at their continuing subordination to the whitestream Canadian state gives rise not only to epidemics of drug addiction and suicide but also to increasingly violent confrontations such as those at Camp Ipperwash (Ontario) and Gustafsen Lake (BC) in the Summer of 1995, not to mention 1990's so-called "Oka crisis" in Quebec.

The contrasting reactions of Canadians to these three crises provide a good indication of how "the aboriginal question" functions politically in Canada today. First, nearly every adult in Canada has some recollection of the Oka crisis, which is situated discursively in terms of the Quebec / Canada conflict. For Canadians, it is a high point of solidarity with First Nations against Quebec in the wake of the collapse of the Meech Lake

---

18 That is, since aboriginal objections to the Meech Lake Accord acquired prominence as one good reason why Canadians should resist recognizing Quebec as a "distinct society". On the history of that particular debate, see Cohen (1990) and Fournier (1990).

accord. For francophone Quebecers, it is a low point that has been poisoning the Quebec / First Nations relationship and playing into the hands of the Canadians. And for members of First Nations, it is at once a high point in their political / cultural affirmation and struggle for recognition as well as a bitter example of Canada's willingness to use force (in this case, both police and the army) against them.

At Oka, I should note, the armed confrontation between Mohawks from the Kanesatake community[19] and the Sûreté du Québec led to the death of a police officer. For several weeks in the course of summer 1990, outrage was extreme among Canadians at the way Quebec was treating aboriginal people, and in particular at the racist excesses of the Sûreté du Québec. What of Ipperwash and Gustafsen Lake? Well, in preparing to write these lines, I myself had difficulty remembering the name of the place in Ontario where, just a few months before, an aboriginal protestor was shot and killed by the Ontario Provincial Police; and I had to double-check the spelling of "Gustafsen" Lake, where four aboriginal protesters were injured (two of them seriously)[20] in the confrontation with the Royal Canadian Mounted Police (RCMP). (In writing this on the other hand, "Kanesatake," flowed fairly spontaneously from fingers to keyboard.)

The two 1995 events attracted a fair degree of attention at the time, but faded from the picture almost as soon as the confrontations were over; and they attracted nowhere near the degree of sympathy among Canadians that the Kanesatake Mohawks obtained in a flash. In fact, as each of these 1995 confrontations erupted, the aboriginal protesters were branded as extremists, terrorists, criminals, thugs, even "native fascists."[21] Questions about police methods, even after the deaths of and injuries to aboriginals, were muted to say the least. One argument, in 1995, was that native "communities struggle to control renegades who answer to no one."[22] Whereas at Oka the Warriors were fighting the good fight, five years later they had evolved into selfish, dangerous, out-of-control "rogues" who do not even recognize

---

19 Several of the key players among the Mohawk "Warriors" were, in fact, from outside Kanesatake, a number of them, in fact, having been more or less kicked out of the other Mohawk community of Akwesasne. But this is not the point: the fight was on behalf of the Kanesatake community. On the Oka crisis, see York and Pindera (1991).

20 "A time to Decolonize, not Dismantle Canada," *Canadian Dimension*, Dec. 1995 - Jan. 1996, p.5.

21 For examples of such labelling, see William Johnson, "'Warriors' no more than native fascists," *The Edmonton Journal* (EJ), 5 August 1995; and Joan Bryden, "Rogue Warriors; The heroic image of native warriors is deteriorating as communities struggle to control renegades who answer to no one," EJ, 13 August 1995. For analysis and critique of the stigmatizing, see Steve Hume, "From resistance comes heroes," EJ, 18 September 1995 and Tony Hall, "Who Killed Dudley George? Reflections on Ipperwash and Gustafsen Lake", *Canadian Dimension*, Dec. 1995 - Jan. 1996, p.8-12.

22 Bryden, "Rogue Warriors".

band authority. Someone reading Quebec's French language press in 1990 would have been familiar with this talk, for the Warriors were already deeply controversial in the communities where they were active. The French-language media wasted no time in using this information to delegitimize the Kanesatake Warriors; the English-language media were more interested in reporting how the French-language press was negative in its coverage of the Warriors, thereby pointing to the racism of their francophone colleagues.[23]

In 1995, with no Quebec / Canada angle overdetermining their coverage of events, Canadian media spontaneously surrendered to the temptation of immediately labelling the protests in Ontario and BC as criminal, terrorist, fascist. *The Globe and Mail*'s editorializing on the initiation of Joseph Peters made the same point: Canadians should not be too quick to accept self-government because who knows what aboriginal radicals will do with it. Canadian reporters, editors, columnists, and editorial writers were now ready to hear the stories of native internal divisions, of young radicals ignoring the authority of elected Chiefs and band councils, and of troubling traditional practices.

The fact is that internal divisions among native communities between elected band councils and chiefs and their supporters on the one hand, and other groups more insistent on traditional forms of aboriginal authority and political process on the other, are decades old; they stem directly from the subordination of indigenous peoples to the Canadian state and its imposition of a whitestream system of government, against aboriginal systems.[24] The Canadian media found out about this, but somehow only well after Oka.

One key target of this book, in this perspective, is the role played by the media in the formation, not only of "public opinion", but of our very identities as members of (among other things) nations. In a society such as Canada, most of the information circulating about public issues not only goes through the media but is shaped by them. At every step of on-going political discussions, the media reinforce their audience's identification with dominant interests by distributing prominent attention to actors according to the importance they themselves assign, and by adopting as their own the discursive categories promoted by dominant actors.

As Ericson, Baranek, and Chan show, "[t]he news-media institution is pivotal to the ability of authorities to make convincing claims" (1991: 8). The news-media do this by appearing to be neutral. But the news, like the law, is a "disciplinary and normalizing discourse", concerned with *"policing*, defined in the original French sense, as a mechanism for the moral health and improvement of the population … In the process of policing, law and news articulate public morality" (Ericson, Baranek and Chan, 1991: 7).

---

23 On the Oka crisis as primarily a media event, see Morris (1995).

24 On these general issues, see Boldt (1993) and Frideres (1988).

Media audiences *may* resist this discourse of the media through their own interpretive activity, but the existence of such a culture of discursive resistance is always highly problematic (see Tester, 1994); as far as national identities in Canada are concerned, there is no such resistance worth speaking of. These may seem like rather bald assertions, with little to recommend them. I hope to show in these pages that the media are indeed a crucial player in the re/production of national / colonial identities in Canada today; and that they do so by making themselves a diligent auxiliary of state institutions such as the courts and police. Indeed, Ericson and his co-authors go so far as to say that the news is an agency of social control and an integral part of the processes of crime, law, and justice.

● ● ●

It is becoming clear that, when the Quebec-related issues are put aside, there is nothing like a consensus among Canadians on a just settlement of aboriginal claims. While this dissensus is often interpreted as a gathering backlash among Canadians against First Nation claims,[25], it is more likely that the resistance was there all along, hidden from view by the anti-Quebec alliance. Indeed, the so-called backlash has not made the slightest dent in Canadian solidarity with the Cree of northern Quebec: the same person can enthusiastically come to the defence of the James Bay Cree and adopt a hard line on any number of aboriginal claims in English Canada.

In British Columbia, for example, there is permanent controversy over what is known as "the Nisga'a claim." Up until 1991, the BC government always refused to negotiate treaties with any native people.[26] Since the late nineteenth century, north-western BC's Nisga'a people have been trying to obtain recognition of their title to roughly 25,000 square kilometers of land. They got nowhere until 1973 when a court decision that went against them was written in such a way as to provide a political victory. The resulting instability prompted the federal government to start negotiations, which were blocked by the BC government until the early 1990s.

In the fall of 1995, the federal and BC governments finally proposed a settlement to the Nisga'a. Negotiations were concluded in February 1996 with a treaty in which the Nisga'a obtain title to about 8% of the land in their original claim, logging rights over some further land, financial compensation, and political autonomy amounting to a form of municipal government.

---

25 As a prime example of the backlash, see Melvin H. Smith's book *Our Home or Native Land* (1995).

26 There are a few minor exceptions, but approximately one hundred native bands have been unable to obtain any kind of settlement with the BC government, for claims that cover a large majority of the province's territory. Settlement of the Nisga'a claim is seen as marking the beginning of the end of this situation.

TABLE I.I – *Three models of aboriginal government*

	Sechelt / Nisga'a	AFN (Charlottetown)	Alberta Treaty Chiefs, Mohawk
WITHIN CANADIAN CONSTITUTION	yes	yes	no
SELF–GOVERNMENT	municipal	prov. / fed.	prov. / fed.
APPLICATION OF CANADIAN CHARTER	yes	no	no
LAWS OF GENERAL APPLICATION	yes	no	no
JUSTICE SYSTEM	minor offences	wider	wider

They also agreed to surrender their exemption from income taxes and gave up an important demand to fishing rights which was replaced by a limited side-deal with the federal government. Finally, they agreed to be bound by the Canadian Charter of Rights and Freedoms, and by federal and provincial laws of general application, all of which had been strongly resisted by the Assembly of First Nations and other native groups during the 1992 Charlottetown constitutional negotiations. The AFN model of self-government was itself considered overly moderate by the Alberta Treaty Chiefs and the Mohawk Nation, among others, who boycotted the Charlottetown process and referendum (See Table 1.1).

The Nisga'a, then, obtained a very small part of what they had claimed, not only in terms of amounts of land, resources and autonomy but also in terms of the kind of autonomy and right to self-government. And this is at a time when the federal government claims to be recognizing "inherent right" (see Government of Canada, 1995). If something like the initiation of Joseph Peters takes place on Nisga'a territory after the treaty takes effect, the "victim" will have the exact same recourses as Peters had in 1988. To a large extent, these limits to the Nisga'a gains are due to the very hard line taken by the nominally progressive BC government, which had to deal with public opinion and political opposition little inclined to entertain the notion of substantial aboriginal self-government advocated by the "national" leadership of aboriginal peoples (see Gawthrop, 1996).

Still, as soon as the agreement in principle was announced, the opposition BC Liberal Party declared that it reserved the right, if it won the coming election, to renegotiate the treaty,[27] even to "tear up any deal that gives BC's

---

27 From February 12, 1996, when the agreement in principle was reached, it was expected that two more years would be needed to produce a finalised treaty; a provincial election was to be held no later than October 1996. The election, in fact was held on 28 May 1996.

native Indians special status," because "there has to be an agreement that there is to be one law for all British Columbians."[28] As hard-nosed as the BC government was, its very willingness to come to an agreement depended significantly on the will of the premier, Mike Harcourt, who was about to leave politics just before the election. In that context, wrote Victoria's *Times Colonist*, "the proposed deal is set to become embroiled in a no-holds-barred provincial election – perhaps the dirtiest ever in British Columbia."[29]

As it happened, the Nisga'a accord was a non-issue in the electoral campaign. As the former BC Liberal leader Gordon Gibson commented after the election, both major parties were afraid of the issue, and so they kept it out of the campaign[30]; only the BC Reform party campaigned on the accord, some of its billboards saying "One country, one people, one law."[31] Still, with only the governing NDP supporting the accord, the Liberals obtained 41% of the popular vote and Reform 9%; the New Democrats, with only 39%, retained their hold on government because of the geographical concentration of their support.[32] The Liberals and New Democrats were able to adopt a low profile on the Nisga'a accord because polls indicated that British Columbians thought aboriginal land claims to be entirely unimportant[33]. Thus, while the campaign failed to arouse much overt hostility toward aboriginal peoples, this was accomplished at the price of a bland (but brittle) indifference towards native issues. As far as British Columbians were concerned in the spring of 1996, the status quo so destructive of aboriginal societies could very well go on. By December of 1996, when *Maclean's* magazine conducted its annual year-end opinion poll, all of 1% of Canadians thought that native issues were the most important issue facing Canada; in British Columbia, native issues did not even register.[34]

---

28 Stewart Bell, Mark Hume and Justine Hunter, "Nisga'a treaty sales job begins," *The Vancouver Sun*, 13 February 1996, A1-2. The first quote is from the reporters paraphrasing Liberal leader Gordon Campbell; the second one is a direct quote from Campbell reacting to the announcement of the agreement in principle.

29 "Nisga'a deal a political football," unsigned editorial, *Victoria Times Colonist*, 14 February 1996, A4.

30 On *Politics*, CBC Newsworld, 29 May 1996.

31 I saw this sign on the side of the main road between Kamloops and Jasper in mid-April 1996. One may find something troubling in this slogan of the hard-right Reform party, in its parallel with the Nazi slogan "One people, one party, one leader."

32 The NDP won 39 seats, the Liberals 33 and Reform 2. One seat was won by a start-up party, the Progressive Democratic Alliance. See Ian Haysom, "Clark clings to power," *The Vancouver Sun*, 29 May 1996.

33 Stuart Hunter and Barbara McLintock, "BC poll rates land claims at bottom of concerns," *The Vancouver Sun*, 6 March 1996.

34 See "Future Imperfect," *Maclean's*, 30 December 1996. For the answers to the question "What is the most important problem / issue facing Canada?," see pages 18 and 46.

We are left to conclude from these prominent developments (and many others) that Canadians are favourable to native claims so long as they themselves are not affected, and so long as the claims can be used against Quebec: there should be no cost to Canadians, who should not be expected to change anything about themselves. Thus, as the Nisga'a agreement itself shows, when aboriginal claims are dealt with on their own merits (as opposed to their utility as a Quebec-busting weapon), aboriginal peoples are muscled into agreements that leave colonialism very much in place. In contemporary Canada, this results in the politically common-place and morally abhorrent practice of using someone else to serve one's own dominant position. Quebec has not done much better, unable as it is to go beyond a limited recognition of aboriginal nationhood, but it has the partial excuse of having to defend itself against the Canadian-aboriginal alliance, of which First Nations are the sharply pointed moral emblem. And First Nations, with all the excuses of the world, play opportunist politics, at which they are likely to get burned.

Being Québécois and sympathetic to native claims in their own right, I find all this extraordinarily painful – and, looking at the Canadian part in this, quite repugnant. This book is about working through the anger, reaching for something like what Buddhists call "the void," and thereby taking one step toward "becoming what one is." My point is that native claims will not be taken seriously so long as we, in the white stream, are not willing to see that ending colonialism involves not only a change in the colonized, but also in the colonizer. I have, of course, no great expectation that this will happen in "our" politics: there is no such thing as political liberation. But something like a thought-experiment *is* possible. But don't think, look: what is required is, among other things, looking again (or, perhaps, for once) at our modern criteria of right and wrong; they are constitutive of who we are. In this enterprise, there is much to learn from the ordeal of Joseph Peters.

Chapter 2
Colonialism

For me, it started with two articles in *The Globe and Mail*, about the Joseph Peters case. Then, my interest piqued, I went to the judgement itself, obtained on-line from a friend at the Law Faculty. I read, and re-read the three texts so many times that I knew much of them by heart. A first analysis emerged.

Many, many months later, in the town near which the initiation of Joseph Peters occurred; in the offices of the local newspaper, I am in a backroom, looking through a mess of old issues, bound a year at a time. I am alone in this room; the people across the way ignore me. They write at their computers, banter about local characters who will be in next week's paper, whine jokingly about how political correctness is making it difficult to put descriptive labels on people.

It has been a few years now since the events and the lawsuit. The newsprint is old, dusty, yellowed, slightly brittle with the air of time passed. I find the relevant articles, eleven of them, and suddenly the feel of this story that has been with me for four years changes radically: the extent and atmosphere of the reports make it a story about neighbours. It is here, just up the road, that Joseph Peters was grabbed and initiated. There are still things that are not said in these articles, but in comparison the story as told in *The Globe and Mail* was clearly lifeless, abstracted. Written for a "national audience," it could have been about anyone, anywhere; but, as I sit in this backroom leafing through old papers, that story is not *here*, and it is not about *these* people.

● ● ●

His name was not, as a matter of fact, Joseph Peters: I changed it, along with those of all the men and women involved in this story. I also changed the name of the community, and those of the two community newspapers that reported on the initiation and its aftermath. This is something I have to explain before going ahead with the story of Joseph Peters, his wife, and his initiators. The explanation will at times seem like a technicality of academic research: in a minor sense, it is. But it is much more a reflection on relationships: that between a writer and the individuals whose stories are being told, and that between cultures of unequal power that interact with each other. While academic technicalities approach this in terms of "research ethics," the key word in these relationships is respect. And there is nothing technical about that.

There are traditions in the writing of sociology and anthropology of changing the names of places and of people for at least two purposes. Place names are often changed to indicate that the community studied is somehow typical or representative of a larger social space. Thus, Everett Hughes in his classic study of industrialization and urbanization in Quebec wrote of "Cantonville" as emblematic of what was then called "French Canada" (Hughes, 1943). It was not hard for minimally curious readers to discover that "Cantonville" was in fact Drummondville – this was no big secret, but rather a rhetorical strategy whose vocation was to generalise from Drummondville to the whole of Quebec. This applies to the story of *Peters v. Campbell*: in many ways, it is emblematic of the relationship between whitestream Canada and First Nations.

Preserving the anonymity of research participants – individuals a sociologist has interviewed in the course of her research, for example – is the other reason why names may be changed. In the last few years, North American universities and academic associations have accorded increased importance to overseeing "research ethics," through committees and formal guidelines. Thus, all research projects that involve "human participants" must be approved in advance of their being carried out, by "ethics committees" composed of the researcher's peers. These ethics committees evaluate the propriety of a project on the basis of their university's guidelines which are binding upon the researcher.

The general point of ethics guidelines is that the research participants should not be hurt by the research in any way – physically, morally, emotionally, psychologically, financially; their interests should, in fact, be advanced by the research. As well, they should be fully informed, in advance of their participation, of the purpose and manner of the research and of the use that will be made of their participation. And their privacy must be respected. Once informed of all these things, prospective participants must sign a consent form explaining that they do understand and accept all the implications of their involvement in the research project. Then they can be interviewed, made to jump through hoops, or whatever else the academic doing the research needs them to do.

The principles underlying these ethics procedures are worthy, of course. But the procedures themselves, which are often university-wide, irrespective of the specific experience of various disciplines, are as likely as not to miss the boat. For example – and this is where "Joseph Peters" enters the scene – information that is in "the public domain" can be used in research without the approval of the people involved or the need to respect confidentiality. In a lot of cases, this is sensible enough: if your name is in the newspaper, and this is where I take my information from, I am not revealing anything that was not already known. So there is no need to either obtain your permission or to give you an alias for the sake of anonymity.

But things can be more complicated than that. First of all, what counts as "the public record"? My university's guidelines say that whatever information is ordinarily available to the general public is part of "the public record." Clearly, a newspaper article is included here. But what about a court judgement? That text may well be the newspaper reporter's raw material, and anybody who wants a copy could get it, either by writing to the Clerk of the Court or, as I did, off the internet. But who will *ordinarily* do this? Certainly not your average *Globe and Mail* reader, however one may want to define "average." Does this mean that the judicial decision is not ordinarily *available* to such a person, and that therefore it is not part of "the public record"? Well, there are large amounts of legal scholarship published every day that analyze and comment on judicial texts, on the very ordinary assumption that these texts are part of the public domain – ethics committees in law schools do *not* exercise a mandate over such textual research.

The first problem, of course, is with the very notion of *the* public record, a notion that is predicated on the existence of a "general public": there is no such thing. All publics, and therefore all records, are specialized. Some publics are bigger than others, but they are no less specialized: they have a specific pattern of including / excluding texts, and it is a person's familiarity with the pattern and its general contents that makes her a member of that public. In this sense, a public is in fact an interpretive / imagined community (see Anderson, 1991; and Fish, 1989).

The second complication is that individuals who find themselves in one or another publicly available record may not have wanted to be there. For various reasons, their reticence has not been heeded, and there they are, despite themselves. Should I pay no attention to this, and simply follow the rule that if a piece of information is somehow "public," I can use it? What is the big deal about doing that, you may ask? Forget for a moment the *Peters v. Campbell* situation of colonial domination, and think of the issue as involving your parents' divorce, or yours. Suppose it is a very nasty divorce, in which various family secrets are told in open court and the children are used as pawns by each side's lawyers; suppose also that somewhere a professor of sociology, or law, finds the case interesting and decides to write a book about it, warts and all. Perhaps one parent, or both, deserve the humiliation, but perhaps not; and, surely, the children deserve none of it. It is your family story that is going to be told over two hundred pages. Don't you want to keep this from happening? Or, at the very least don't you want your names to be changed, so that you won't be recognized? Some people, of course, choose to air their family dramas in front of very large audiences; ugly families have been the lifeblood of a large number of day-time talk shows in North America for several years. But that is just the point: these families choose to do this. In court, people do not have a choice over whether their stories will be told.

● ● ●

Let me come back to the case of *Peters v. Campbell*, with not only its ordinary privacy issues, but also with its dimension of colonial domination. All the information presented in this book about this case was already in the public record, as defined by academic guidelines and practice. I uncovered no facts that would have been previously known only to the private individuals involved. The information used here was either published in *The Globe and Mail* ("Canada's national newspaper"), a Western Canadian newsmagazine, and local weekly newspapers; or contained in the text of the Court's decision; or in other government records accessible to anyone who asks.[1] I could have easily retained the participants' real names and respected the letter of academia's research ethics guidelines. Indeed, my first publication on this story contains no aliases, because it had not occurred to me at the time that there might be a problem with using the public record or, in this connection, with that very concept of "public record." (Do not look for that publication in the bibliography: it is not there.)

As it is, I doubt very much that any harm has come, or will come, to those involved in *Peters v. Campbell* as a result of that paper in an academic book which deals for the most part with topics quite removed from West Coast aboriginal peoples. It could easily be argued that, if anything, Campbell and his co-defendants stand to gain from the publication of that paper and of this book; that, more broadly, one result of my analysis is to vindicate not only the defendants' but also the aboriginal perspective on the law, at the expense of the Canadian state. The fact is, however, that Campbell et al. were dragged before the Court; that they only told their story with great reluctance and with as little detail as possible. Had they been given a choice, they would have kept their cultural practices to themselves. Even Joseph Peters, the plaintiff, only wanted part of the story to be told (as we will see later).

---

1   A couple of such records would have had very limited circulation, as will be seen in Chapter 3; they play a small part in the analysis.

Disseminating the story, then, after it was forced out by the Court and after newspapers repeated it (with near immediate obsolescence as to its specifics[2] in the minds of most readers), goes against the thrust of the defendants' conduct at trial. Repeating the story again, in the longer-lasting form of a book aimed at a wider public than those made of legal scholars and anthropologists, could be seen as one more step in the colonizing enterprise, a step made even worse, perhaps, because I know I am taking it while claiming to want to debunk colonialism. The justification for this book – and my excuse, if I need one – is in the perspective I bring to "the facts." Just as Campbell and his friends understood their actions as an initiation, as help being provided to Peters and not as "assault and battery", I understand the story I am telling as an attempt to subvert colonial discourse and institutions. Whether or not I succeed at this enterprise is not for me to say.

It is not a simple thing to leave colonialism behind, for any individual writer no more than for society as a whole. This book is the tentative step in that direction that I may take at this time. And, as will soon become clear, my attitude towards cultural practices such as syewen is more positive than merely (and implausibly) neutral. In the struggle of indigenous peoples against colonial states such as Canada, I doubt that a perspective such as this book's will hurt them.

The least I can do, however, is to avoid repeating the actual names of the individuals involved, and of their specific communities. The lives of Campbell and the others have been more than enough disturbed by the lawsuit; they should be allowed to regain the privacy they never intended to surrender. In these pages, then, I will refer to the town as Islandtown, and to its two weekly newspapers as *The Regional News* and *Photopress*.[3]

In following the "public record's" paper trail, I travelled to Islandtown, and talked with people who had either direct contact with the case or who are generally familiar with the region's legal history[4]; for the sake of respect-

---

2   That is to say, within a couple of days at most, few people will remember such things as the names of those involved, or which First Nation was challenging the common law. But it is likely that many readers will retain something basic from the articles, such as "Indians kidnap and torture one of their own, and claim that they have a Charter right to do it", and insert it in their general sense of aboriginal cultures. A little new statement will have been weaved into their narratives of "Indianness," contributing to their own sense of belonging to a superior civilization. This argument is developed in Chapter 3.

3   References to their articles will be presented as RN and PP, each followed by a number. Thus, "RN 6" is *The Regional News*' sixth article, in chronological order. *The Globe and Mail* published two articles on the *Peters v. Campbell* affair and the newsmagazine *Alberta Report* published one; these articles will be referred to as GM 1, GM 2 and AR 1.

4   I did not conduct interviews with these people, the content of which would have served as primary information for my research. But if a file is to be pulled from a cabinet, or if a pile of old newspapers is to be found, somebody has to get involved to find the file for me or direct me to the room in which the back issues are kept.

ing Campbell et al.'s privacy, it was reassuring to find that, outside their immediate communities, memories of the case and of the people involved were extremely dim or altogether non-existent. As one person at the Court registry told me, "you know, there are a lot of people named Peters around here." She had no idea who Joseph Peters might be.

This story of *Peters v. Campbell* is sufficiently specific in time, place, and detail for someone to go out and uncover the real names and circumstances of those involved. I expect few readers would feel the need to go through such trouble. Some scholars may want to study the judicial decision for their own reasons; this is of course a legitimate purpose.[5]

Some readers who are part of British Columbia's legal community, and a few others, will find the aliases transparent: they know the case. They will not learn anything about the participants they could not have discovered by themselves. My hope is that this will change their understanding of the case, of what "the facts" are, and of how they hang together. If somehow they find a use for this change in their own work, I hope that they will strive to keep the individuals behind the aliases out of it.

● ● ●

Academic "ethics guidelines," then, are inadequate to this case. But arriving at this conclusion has required some thinking about ethical issues, as opposed to mechanically filling out forms and following the guidelines. This goes to the heart of the problem with these procedures: when research really involves delicate ethical issues, it is unlikely that standard cross-discipline (or even discipline-wide) rules will be adequate to deal with them.

Nothing, indeed, can replace the personal ethical judgement of the researcher, a judgement that should be developed along with other "professional" competencies, in graduate school at the latest. In most cases, then, formal ethics procedures are likely to be superfluous. And in some cases, they are harmful: they provide a shortcut to thinking about ethics that may hurt the research or indeed the participants. For if the guidelines can fail to protect privacy when they should, they can also sabotage what should be the straightforward participation of people who will be put off by all the formalities of consent form and confidentiality. Thus, in interviews I conducted (for another project, duly approved by my faculty's ethics committee) in the spring of 1995, participants were scornful of what they considered institutional hypocrisy regarding confidentiality and informed consent. In other cases, when the quality of the relationship with participants (and therefore of their contribution to the research) is highly depen-

---

5 Scholars who need full references should write to me, care of Broadview Press, explaining why they need them, and committing to maintaining the privacy of those involved.

dent on first contact, the formalities can actually be scary and result in a refusal to participate. No one is helped by the necessity of such procedures. Which is not to say, of course, that the researcher should not respect and be grateful to the people who agree to participate in research, and treat their contribution accordingly – and this should find an expression in the finished product beyond the "acknowledgements" page.

It is partly because of the bureaucratic formalities of academic ethics guidelines – magnified in Canada nowadays when a researcher deals with members of indigenous nations – that I have not sought to conduct interviews in preparing this book. I would have liked to interview members of the Salish people in the development of this book, so that, among other reasons, their voices could be heard more directly than they finally are. But I could not bring myself to frame my engagement with them in that documentary bureaucracy, under the pretense that in doing so I was respecting them. Not only is mechanically obeying the ethics guidelines no guarantee of actual respect, but on a personal basis I could not see myself approaching an elder for the first time with a consent form in my hand and asking her to sign it before we really started talking.

The raw materials for the research in this book, therefore, are pre-existing[6] texts that, in various ways, narrate events, actions, and decisions. And each of these texts offers a particular angle on these events and decisions to a particular public. I am not looking at the initiation itself, but rather at accounts of the initiation and the events surrounding it. I am asking how the meaning of the initiation is constituted for these publics. This is important, because social relations between groups (and individuals) are cemented by the circulation of meaning about themselves, each other, and the relationship itself. For example: the material relationship between aboriginal peoples and whitestream Canadians has not changed appreciably in the last decade, but the sense that whitestream Canadians have of the circumstances of aboriginal peoples and of the relationship has been notably transformed,[7] leading to current negotiations on the status of First Nations in Canada.

In *Imagined Communities* (1991 [1983]), a now classic study on "the origin and spread of nationalism," Benedict Anderson showed how the development of newspapers (and of the novel as a literary form) played a key role the rise of nations in the nineteenth century. The newspaper is at once highly individualizing, through the experience of reading, and community-forming, by making available to newly literate reading publics information that is uniquely relevant to them. As such, it has contributed immensely to

---

6   In the sense that they were not created through the research process, contrary to interview transcripts for example.

7   This includes, of course, the role that First Nations are seen as playing in the Canadian struggle against Quebec nationalism.

the constitution of national imagined communities, the borders of which are at once linguistic, cultural, and materially inscribed. Newspapers and novels still play this role, and they have been mightily supplemented in the twentieth century by radio, television, and cinema.

Thus, recognition of media personalities can be a good indicator of a reader / viewer's national identity. Few Canadians outside Quebec would know who Bernard Derome is, although he has been TV news anchor for twenty-five years on Radio-Canada, while few francophone Quebecers would know Peter Gzowski, of CBC Radio's Morningside: both men are national institutions, although very little-known outside their respective national community. In the same vein, the sense conveyed to readers of *The Globe and Mail*, *The Regional News*, and *Photopress* about aboriginal peoples and how different they are from "us," is crucially constitutive of the relationship between whitestream Canada and First Nations, and indeed of who "we" are, collectively and individually. Exploring and challenging this sense is largely what this book is about.

● ● ●

Textual research strategy or not, though, there are still difficulties. Anthropologist Marie Françoise Guédon has found in her work with the Dene people, that elders "would not refuse to reveal anything of their practices to anyone who is clearly able to at least keep a neutral but open attitude in the matter" (Guédon, 1994: 57). And, in the past, anthropologists have also obtained the cooperation of people of the Coast Salish nation in observing both Potlatches and Winter Dances (see for instance Suttles, 1987). But it is also the case that elders in a number of situations have been reluctant to speak openly of important practices (see J. Couture, 1991).

In repeating testimony from the *Peters v. Campbell* lawsuit, I am not disclosing anything new about the existence or details of the cultural practices involved in Peters's initiation; they are already well-known among students of West Coast peoples.[8] But part of the story I tell was voiced by specific individuals who felt they were being forced to do so by colonial authorities. Indeed, soon after Peters launched his lawsuit, a locally prominent member of the Salish community issued a press release complaining about the media's lack of respect for their culture in this story; he added that the band's reluctance to speak about it was related to the decades-long ban on the practice of Potlatch, of which syewen is a component. Because of the old ban, they "now guard their traditions closely" (RN 6). A local chief had made the same point only weeks earlier about the Winter Dance: "that is a part of our culture that we'll guard quite closely" (RN 1).

---

8   On ethnographic descriptions of syewen, see Suttles (1987 [1960]: 199-208).

Further, I could not help feeling some unease reading, for example, some anthropological descriptions of the Winter Dance, at the effect of the very flat ethnographic descriptive style. Being flat – something like "the first dancer got up, put on a hat, went to the centre of the room, spun around three times and returned to his seat; the second dancer…"[9] – the description is devoid of the symbolic content with which participants imbue their actions, and this rhetoric can easily seem disrespectful. The writer may not intend the description to be disrespectful, but the people described often will feel it so, and the outside reader may be pulled toward finding the practice absurd because of the "disenchanting"[10] nature of ethnographic description.

I cannot be certain that my own account will entirely avoid this pitfall. I have tried to describe syewen as little as possible, and when I have done so it is with the specific intent of challenging derogatory whitestream notions of aboriginal cultures. In this connection, I hope that Longhouse members who read this will bear with me through some language they may not like; the rough patches are moments on a journey that I have intended as leading to greater respect not only for aboriginal peoples in general but more specifically for practices such as syewen, which whitestream Canadians are likely to have the most trouble accepting.

A few weeks after visiting the local courthouse and the offices of *The Regional News*, I met a man, a member of the Longhouse, from a village some seventy kilometers from Islandtown. Upon hearing of my plans, he immediately told me that this would be badly received because syewen always ends up being presented as "savage." He also hastened to say that syewen is not a religion. After some further dialogue, he agreed to talk again, and to introduce me to other members of the Longhouse if I travelled to his village. I saw him again the next day, and gave him a copy of this chapter's first draft.

I was, of course, very glad for this contact. But what would this do to my plan of working strictly from documentation and not waving consent forms into people's faces? It occured to me that my dialogue with these members of the Longhouse would not fit under the academic definition of "research with human subjects": I would be consulting these men and women in the same spirit as when I show a draft chapter to colleagues and ask them for feedback. They are the experts on syewen and, by responding to my text,

---

9 This particular description is my own invention, for the sake of illustration; it has nothing to do with the Winter Dance.

10 I mean this as closely analogous to the sense in which Max Weber wrote of the rise of instrumental rationality at the expense of substantive rationality as producing a "disenchantment of the world." The literature of the problematic relationship of the anthropologist to the people s/he studies is considerable; I will only note, in connection with the problem of "representation" to be discussed below, the art critic Craig Owens's (1992) discussion in "Improper Names."

they would help me formulate my story in ways that they would not find disrespectful. In this sense, the Longhouse members would not be "participants" in my research, but rather experts, advisers providing feedback.

This construction of the role of the Longhouse members in my research is convenient, of course. But it is more than that: it is a recognition that the real experts on issues such as syewen are the practitioners themselves and that, without losing the spirit of critical inquiry, it is incumbent upon me to produce an account that can stand the test of their evaluation.

Unfortunately, this consultation with Longhouse members did not happen: after talking with people in his community, my contact found that no one wanted to talk to an outsider about syewen. He expressed a willingness to talk to me, but was extremely busy and in the end could not make time for conversations that he clearly felt were a low priority. Meeting him, though, had an impact: whenever I found myself wondering about my narration of the story, I thought of him and of how he would react to this or that depiction. He has kept me on my toes.

● ● ●

It would be most unfortunate if the textual research strategy I have adopted is understood as a denial of aboriginal peoples' right to speak for themselves. My decision stems directly from a concern to answer the question: How can I, in the circumstances of this project, best respect the rights of First Nations peoples? More fundamentally, there is no getting around the fact that I am writing this book as a non-aboriginal person; whatever interviews I might have conducted would still have been filtered by me before finding their way into print. The issue becomes, then, one of my entitlement to do this book at all.

It has, I think, become somewhat well-known to various publics outside aboriginal communities and anthropological circles that aboriginal people are fed up with being studied by (primarily) white academics. And the first half of the 1990s has seen these academics taken to task for claiming to speak for aboriginal people, at the same time that the latter have found unprecedented outlets for speaking their point of view to whitestream publics. But this does not have to mean that white academics should be silenced, or should silence themselves. Thus, in the Foreword to *In Celebration of Our Survival: The First Nations of British Columbia*, a 1991 issue of the journal BC *Studies* otherwise authored entirely by aboriginal writers, artists, and activists, editor Allan Smith wrote that the journal "remains convinced that investigators of competence and sensitivity can contribute constructively to discussion of a society or culture whether they are affiliated with it or not" (Smith in Jensen and Brooks, 1993 [1991]: 3).

This issue is an important one, both in political terms and in theoretical terms. It is worth exploring in some detail, for it goes well beyond arguments about political correctness. Also keep in mind that this book is not an anthropological study of an aboriginal people, but rather an essay on the Canada-First Nations relationship and on what Canadian modernity has to learn from First Nations. This is a concern that permeates the whole of the book, but that will become most evident in the last two chapters, which have little to say about the initiation of Joseph Peters specifically; they have, on the other hand, a lot to say about those shortcomings of modernity which are brought into sharp relief by the world in which syewen is practised.

Whitestream modernity's ways of life and of thinking are vastly different from aboriginal ways – from aboriginality – to a degree rarely acknowledged or even grasped by people reared in whitestream ways. These differences are so deep that it has been possible to speak of them as involving "irreconcilable or irreducible elements of human relations" (Turpel, 1990: 13). This is a notion familiar to western philosophy at least since Wittgenstein's *Philosophical Investigations* (1968 [1953]) and, in fact, since what is often called the cultural relativism of Herder. Practically, for the purposes of this study, this means that whatever understanding of aboriginal ways I may obtain will be a "western" understanding: understanding aboriginality will depend on its *redescription*[11] in occidental terms. Recognizing this is a basic theoretical condition of possibility for inter-cultural communication; it is not an apology for intruding on an other culture's terrain.

Redescribed through "western" eyes, aboriginal ways will necessarily be distorted; there is no escaping this. Some would conclude that people not possessed of an aboriginal point-of-view have no option but to be silent, that any attempt to account for aboriginal ways in occidental terms is cultural appropriation, doing violence to aboriginal people. Contrary to its ostensible politics, I believe this view to be politically inimical to aboriginal interests. It is also theoretically reductionist and simplistic. I will not argue this latter claim at great length here, but I hope to show it to be correct in the course of analyzing the *Peters v. Campbell* story.

Still, two things should be noted. First, one should be clear about the theoretical problem presented by the fact of writing about a group other than one's own. Both poles of the theoretical difficulty have been nicely identified by the art critic Craig Owens (1992) as involving Marx and Foucault. Speaking of small-holding French peasants in the middle of the nineteenth century, Marx wrote that "they cannot represent themselves,

---

11 I prefer this word to the ordinarily used *translation*, because of the latter's connotation of neutrality: if we translate from one language to another, one might expect a correspondence, and a *thing* as referent which can arbitrate between a good and a bad translation. Speaking of redescription, on the other hand, foregrounds the fact that we were dealing with particular descriptions in the first place, and we are routinely involved in processes of moving from one to another.

they must be represented";[12] not that he thought to represent them: he was explaining how it was that a dictatorship could establish itself with the support of peasants. His point was that the material circumstances of peasants made them unable to speak for themselves, such that it was likely that someone else – in this case the dictator Louis Napoléon Bonaparte – would claim to speak and act politically for them.[13] A century later, in the context of "the contemporary critique of representation", Jacques Deleuze would remark to Michel Foucault, "In my opinion, you were the first ... to teach us something absolutely fundamental: the indignity of speaking for others" (quoted in Owens, 1992: 262).[14] The issue here is the same as that studied by Marx: an analysis of the political effects of measures taken by "people who claim to be representative and who make a profession of speaking for others, in the name of others..." (Deleuze in Foucault, 1994E: 309; my translation). In both cases, the claim to speak for others is self-serving, and injurious to the "represented" others who, let us remember, cannot speak and be heard.[15]

I am certainly not claiming to speak for aboriginal people in this book. And, while they have for a long time been silenced in whitestream Canada, this is no longer the case: their voices are being heard to an increasing degree, not only politically but also intellectually and artistically. In some ways, I am clearly writing about them; but I believe it would be more accurate to say that I am writing about us and them, and that in fact I am writing in a spirit of dialogue with them. It is in this sense, to take an obvious example, that an engagement will be found in these pages with the work of aboriginal activists, scholars, and artists such as Joseph Couture, Ron Hamilton, Lee Maracle, Ovide Mercredi, Georges Sioui, and Mary-Ellen Turpel. In this perspective, I believe that the challenge for a non-aboriginal person is not of summoning the self-control to keep quiet, but rather of finding ways to approach such issues "in the right spirit", as James Tully (1995: 19) wrote in a serious attempt to do just that.

Suffice it to say, second, that a call to silence does not serve First Nations because of the inescapable reality that, in Canada as elsewhere, they must live surrounded by a large majority of "whites." As one man noted, who

---

12 In *The Eighteenth Brumaire of Louis Bonaparte* (1852), quoted in Owens (1992:261).

13 For this account of Marx's 1852 analysis of French peasants, I am relying on Marx (1963: 310–329).

14 That dialogue between Deleuze and Foucault was published in 1972 as "Les intellectuels et le pouvoir," in *L'Arc*. It is reproduced as Foucault (1994E), in which Owens's quote of Deleuze is at p.309.

15 In the Deleuze / Foucault dialogue, the "others" spoken about are the inmates of France's prisons, whom Foucault had been trying to help get their own words out to the French people, saying that living conditions in prison were intolerable. On Foucault's creation of the Groupe d'intervention sur les prisons, see Eribon (1990).

participated in the Assembly of First Nation's 1992 parallel constitutional process, and who is quoted in the Commissioners' Report: "We must live in the white man's world. We can never go back and live the way our ancestors lived. But the values and beliefs – we can hang on to them. Believe in that; *practise* that" (Wallace Fox, in Commissionners' Report, 1992: 1; emphasis added).

Independent of issues of rights, the circumstances of aboriginal peoples could not but be improved if whitestream society acquired a better understanding of aboriginal ways and discovered, in fact, that it has something to learn from them. With or without aboriginal self-government, communication between peoples should be a considerable asset to First Nations. Although the redescription inherent to such intercultural communication always involves distortions, the degree and character of distortion will vary. Some distortions are grosser than others, and some may be injurious while others may not. Thus, several occidental readings, or redescriptions, of aboriginal ways are possible and the character of these readings will largely depend on the spirit in which each reader approaches aboriginal cultures.

Judicial decisions are one type of reading, which typically have involved gross distortions of, and severe injury to, aboriginal ways. In one sense, this is because, as Turpel (1990) writes, courts do not take cultural difference seriously; they subsume aboriginal concepts under whitestream legal language. But an occidental reader who approaches aboriginal ways in a spirit of sympathy and good will, and who looks at aboriginal concepts as equal to his own, can contribute to a better relationship between cultures. Of course, aboriginal women and men also address whitestream audiences – now more than ever before, but however they do so the audience will interpret what it hears according to its own frame of reference.

Overall, a better understanding of aboriginal cultures by members of whitestream culture may be produced through the process of making these multiple readings, and of cross-referencing them, as it were, among readers of good will. This is, I think, in keeping with the outlook advocated by Turpel:

> When we think of cultural differences between Aboriginal peoples and the Canadian state and its legal system, we must think of these as problems of conceptual reference for which there is no common grounding or authoritative foothold. Necessarily, we can't 'decide' the substance of cultural differences from a position of a particular institutional and conceptual cultural framework; each culture is capable of sensitivity to the basic condition of difference, and should develop cross-cultural relations accordingly. (Turpel, 1990: 14)

I have therefore endeavoured to participate in the process of reading the relationship between aboriginal peoples and whitestream Canada, in the knowledge that I can only do so from an occidental perspective. We will see, however, that while perspectives are incommensurable and no "common grounding" is available, no perspective is entirely fixed or unchangeable. This is something that, in theoretical terms, Wittgenstein and poststructuralist theory (and Herder, for that matter) would recognize.[16]

There is not only the spirit of the approach that matters, of course. Becoming familiar with aboriginal concepts, forms of life and expression, is at least as important. And it is very difficult to achieve. The members of the Royal Commission on Aboriginal Peoples, for instance, write at the completion of their massive research and conversation with aboriginal women and men, "It would be presumptuous to suggest that we have come to understand Aboriginal world view, or that we could adequately represent in these pages the complexity and diversity of Aboriginal cultures" (Canada, 1996A: 616). In a similar way, Rupert Ross writes that he "had no idea how big an issue (he) was flirting with" (1996: 101) when he first published an account (in 1992) of a sexually abused Ojibway woman's decision to tell her story in Ojibway rather than English. He now knows that he then knew next to nothing, and that still today he is nowhere near a comprehensive understanding.

I have no doubt that I understand very little of aboriginal ways in general and Coast Salish practices in particular. There is no question that, in my reading of the Coast Salish relationships at work in the *Peters v. Campbell* conflict, I am missing a lot of things.[17] But the issue is not whether I get everything; it is, rather, that I get enough to show the injustice in whitestream practices toward aboriginal peoples. I have wagered, in writing this book, that I do get enough to achieve that purpose; and, while I have tried hard to weed out inadvertent misreadings, I can only hope that I have suceeded.[18]

Practically, aboriginal perspectives have been and continue to be affected and transformed, usually for the worse, by their contact with the white stream; occidental perspsectives could well afford to be affected by aboriginal practices. This is why I have sought to emulate Michel Foucault's yearn-

---

16 On Wittgenstein (besides his *Philosophical Investigations*), see Easton (1983); on poststructuralism, see Weedon (1987); on Herder, see Young (1995).

17 On the difficulty for a non-aboriginal person to read aboriginal con/texts, see also R.A. Williams (1992).

18 Note that the test that would decide on success / failure is not a theoretical one, nor even an evaluation on some measurable scale of how much I know about aboriginality. The test is a pragmatic one, of whether or not readers of this book do rethink their sense of whitestream / aboriginal practices (no matter what conclusion they eventually reach).

ing to "penser autrement qu'on ne pense et percevoir autrement qu'on ne voit". For Foucault, this is a quest that defines philosophical practice today: "... au lieu de légitimer ce qu'on sait déjà, (la philosophie aujourd'hui ne consiste-t-elle pas) à entreprendre de savoir comment et jusqu'où il serait possible de penser autrement?" (Foucault, 1984: 14, 15).

Chapter 3
Individual freedom

Winter on Vancouver Island is wonderfully mild by Canadian standards. Temperatures rarely fall below zero degree celsius, snow is even more unusual, and in Victoria the notoriously fragile cherry blossoms begin to bloom by mid-February. Still, it is not the kind of weather that would generally prompt people to undress and jump naked in a creek – which is one of the things that was forced upon Joseph Peters during his initiation. Add to this that his initiators bit him, dug their fingers into his sides, and hit him with tree branches. Testifying at the trial, he told the Court that the beatings were severe enough that he screamed in pain and that his skin, in various places, was marked, lacerated, and that welts were raised. As I have already noted, he was not given any food over a period of four days, and very little water.

Before going any further, let us note how this description of the initiation would be found offensive by members of the Long House. Drawn from Judge Hood's decision, it is stripped of the spiritual context that would endow it with meaning. Some of this context is recovered by Pamela Amoss's account of the worldview of the Nooksack people, an ancestral branch of the Coast Salish people. Amoss writes that, in order to function appropriately in society and in the natural environment,

> … a person needed to establish lines of communication with the non-human realm. He would do so through a vision encounter with a more or less individualized, personalized manifestation of the power which pervaded the wild realm of nature. The passage from the human sphere to the nonhuman sphere was ritually dangerous and hedged with taboos. Contact could be achieved only if the human supplicant were purged of the taint of human existence. Bathing cleaned off the smell of sweat and the odor of smoke from the plank houses; fasting and emetics cleaned out all trace of food from the belly; isolation in wild

and desolate places protected the seeker from the contamination of
human companionship. (Amoss, 1978: 12, 13)

Here, the previous description's words (beating, biting, starving) are
replaced by words such as purge, clean, protect. The first description leads
naturally to other words, belonging to the legal language of common law:
assault, battery, false imprisonment. In the second description, the concepts
of the common law find no foothold; the events described refer primarily to
the relationship of one person with the nonhuman realm, with social relationships taking a backseat. Although syewen is not an exact repetition of
pre-contact Nooksack rituals, it is very much the case that a contemporary
initiation is primarily concerned with making a connection with the nonhuman realm, an important difference being the active part played by other
individuals, the initiators, in the calling-on of the vision.

In later chapters, we will return to the specifically spiritual import of
syewen and to the changes such rituals have undergone since contact. For
now, it is important to note how the Coast Salish and the whitestream
descriptions of events such as the initiation of Joseph Peters focus on different dimensions: the spiritual dimension for one, and the social dimension for
the other (See Graph 3.1). And while the social dimension is present but
secondary in the Coast Salish description, the spiritual dimension is not even
recognized in the whitestream description.

Let us now focus on the social dimension, and look at what Canadians
are made to see of the initiation of Joseph Peters.

● ● ●

In the course of reporting the Supreme Court of British Columbia's decision in Peters v. Campbell, The Globe and Mail[1] outlines the circumstances that
lead to the suit, recounting testimony documenting (A) the initiate's lack of
consent to the initiation and (B) the physical injuries and humiliations that
he sustained:

(A) he was "forcibly taken" to the Long House, "imprisoned," "forced
to undergo the initiation ceremonies"; he "did not authorize anyone to have
him initiated as a spirit dancer and was not interested in learning about his
people's culture";

(B) the initiators "took turns digging their fingers into his stomach area
and biting him on his sides," causing superficial injuries whose existence was
confirmed by the physician who treated Joseph Peters upon his escape; "…
he was stripped naked, forced to walk backwards into the water and sub-

---

1   Coverage of the story in Western Report was very similar to that of The Globe and Mail, not only
in content but also in general tone. For the sake of brevity, I will generally stick to The Globe's
coverage.

merge himself three times, he told the court. He said he was then beaten with cedar branches"; during these four days, he was given no food and very little water.

GRAPH 3.1 — *Initiations: Social and Spiritual Dimensions*

COAST SALISH DESCRIPTION

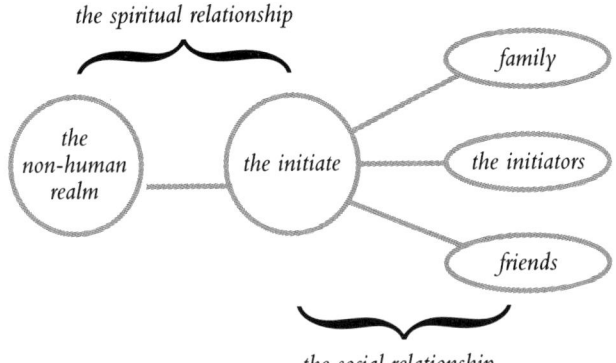

WHITESTREAM DESCRIPTION

Other features of the initiation's circumstances could have been identified by the reporter in his attempt to provide readers with an understanding of the events which could have been narrated in a manner more respectful of Coast Salish culture. But the story he does tell anchors firmly Joseph Peters's grievance in one of modernity's fundamental narratives, at least as it relates to men: the autonomy of the self expressed as an inalienable human right.

The philosopher Charles Taylor writes that "(t)o talk of universal, natural, or human rights is to connect respect for human life and integrity with the notion of autonomy ... And this expresses a central feature of the modern Western moral outlook" (Taylor, 1989: 12).[2] For us, understanding the story of Joseph Peters will require a discussion and analysis of how key narratives of liberal modernity are activated by the initiation and its narration by the Court and the media. We will have to consider the issues of individual autonomy, avoidance of cruelty, due process, humane treatment of "deviants." And in Chapter 6 we will look at the issue of (especially religious)

2   Eloquent in its defence of what is best in modernity and honest in its description of modern limitations, Taylor's work will be used here as a standard-bearer of the modern outlook. Not that Taylor is the last word on what modernity is or stands for, but he does articulate the key strands of what it means to be modern. Things get complicated, and especially debatable, in his account of where these strands come from and how they hang together.

pluralism and the separation of church and state.

In whitestream society, it is taken for granted that men are autonomous selves, with control over the integrity of their body. As such, the fact that Joseph Peters is a man is certainly not unrelated to this other fact that his forced initiation became an affair, an event that quickly acquired the public profile of something outrageous, requiring and receiving both media and judicial attention. To Peters, the override of his consent appeared outrageous, as did the "ordeal" (to quote Judge Hood) to which he was subjected. It was no more acceptable to the Court, or to *The Globe and Mail* (as the news report suggested and the editorial made crystal clear) and *Western Report*. Indeed, nobody thought to tell Joseph Peters that his "no" really meant "yes."

Now, this underscores the fact that the extent to which women are autonomous selves remains an issue, and especially so when it comes to control over the integrity of their bodies. As was alluded to in the Introduction, this is in fact a very important and obscured part of the story, to which we will return later in this chapter and in further detail in Chapters 4 and 5. Any modernist account – that is to say, for example, the vast majority of whitestream societies' media output – of these events would have to focus on the facts that Joseph Peters was denied the exercise of his free will, and that the autonomy and integrity of his body were violated. But women, and aboriginal women more than others, see their consent routinely violated as they are subjected to treatments far worse than what Joseph Peters experienced. And, routinely also, these other "ordeals" do not make their way to court.

There are some circumstances in which modernity will allow denials and violations of the rights of men, such as with convicted criminals (who, by definition, are rightfully imprisoned) and individuals who are deemed mentally incompetent to make their own decisions.[3] But one of the stories modernity likes to tell about itself is that it has evolved a severe restriction on the infliction of pain and suffering for socially normative purposes.[4] One would not expect that the dominant modern culture would tolerate it coming from the oppressed aboriginal culture.

As Judge Hood put it, Joseph Peters "did suffer injuries, both physical and mental" and he "did experience pain and suffering during his ordeal and for sometime thereafter" (162). Hence the award of compensatory damages.

---

3 Thus, it is possible under Canadian law for family members to have an individual declared mentally incompetent and institutionalized without his or her consent; and "treatment" – say, electroshocks – has often included the infliction of pain and suffering (see A. Alan Borovoy, *When Freedoms Collide: The Case for Our Civil Liberties*, Toronto, Lester & Orpen Dennys, 1988; in particular, Ch. 9 on "Involuntary Civil Confinement"). I hope it is clear that I am not endorsing, here, any such "treatment"; rather, I am outlining some of the suspensions of rights that are deemed acceptable by the dominant occidental criteria.

4 For a critical look at that narrative, see Foucault (1975).

In assessing damages, the court easily came to the conclusion that the intentions of the defendants were good, that "they honestly and sincerely believe in the Dancing Tradition, that they were helping the plaintiff..." (162). As a result, they were not assessed punitive damages. But these good intentions were of no help in getting the suit dismissed.

In deciding the case, as far as the Court was concerned, "the motives of the defendants are irrelevant" (159). It is a curiously interesting fact, however, that Judge Hood referred to the initiation as an "ordeal," a word which I have been foregrounding in previous paragraphs. Now, in addition to its ordinary meaning of some kind of awful experience, "ordeal" carries the historically prior meaning of "a primitive form of trial to determine guilt or innocence by subjecting the accused person to fire, poison, or other serious danger, the result being regarded as a divine or preternatural judgement."[5] Judge Hood's probably unintentional (but who knows?) evocation of a different form of judicial process – which modernity considers "primitive" – does raise, in its own buried way, the issue of the defendants' motives.

So far as we can tell from *The Globe and Mail*'s report and editorial (and also from the judgement itself), Joseph Peters had not done anything to deserve such treatment, and nothing indicates that he was somehow mentally incompetent. On this issue of initiators' motivation, in fact, the reporter's account turns bizarre: almost as an afterthought, he writes that an elder (and defendant) testified that Pat Michaels, Peters's then common-law wife, "had requested that he be initiated as a way of dealing with marital and other problems."

The initiation, a four-day ritual involving fasting and injuries, none of which Joseph Peters consented to, is to be justified on vague grounds of "marital and other problems". Some people have died from such initiations, as *The Globe*'s editorial noted.[6] Could any modern reader of *The Globe and Mail* feel anything but solidarity with Joseph Peters? Could any such reader conclude anything other than that he was assaulted, battered and wrongfully imprisoned? Such a dramatic slant in a news report would seem to go against the rules of reporting to which the prestigious *Globe and Mail* subscribes: balance, readers are routinely told, is required. Now, how does one obtain "balance"? In 1977, the Canadian Daily Newspaper Publishers Association adopted a "Statement of Principles," which requires that the news be presented "comprehensively, accurately and fairly." It defines fairness as "a balanced presentation of the relevant facts in a news report, and of all substantial

---

5 *Webster's Encyclopedic Unabridged Dictionary of the English Language* (New York, Portland House, 1989) 1013; emphasis added.

6 More on the lethal consequences of some initiations later in this chapter.

opinions in a matter of controversy. It precludes distortion of meaning by over- or under-emphasis, by placing faces or quotations out of context…"[7]

The question here is: what counts as "the news"? Is it the initiation of Joseph Peters? Or the judgement by the Supreme Court of British Columbia? Depending on how one answers, "the relevant facts" and context will change. And it is not so simple as to call for "the other side" to be heard – for, indeed, "the other side" is heard in the report, through the (interviewed) voice of the defendant's lawyer, Lara Skye. To this extent, the *Globe and Mail* reporter did his job well. However, presenting two sides in this way, constructing binary oppositions, is part of the difficulty, inasmuch as it is a forceful invitation to take sides. And if the two sides are presented unevenly, a strong moral message is sent about each of them and therefore about ourselves. We will come back to Skye's comments below, but for now the point is this: in order to provide us with an alternative story, the reporter would have needed to do something that the court would not, that is, take seriously the motivations of the initiators. Why didn't he?

The initiators' motivations, clearly, are part of the context of the initiation of Joseph Peters; in neglecting them, and thereby presenting the initiation without an important element of its context, the reporter could be said to have breached the "Statement of Principles." But it is very unclear whether the motivations are part of the context of the judgement: if we believe the judge, they are irrelevant. The reporter had to report on the news (and its context); the news, here, was the Court's decision, not the initiation itself. The decision was that the individual rights of Peters were upheld against aboriginal collective rights and that the motivation of the initiators was irrelevant.

To go beyond this, the reporter would have needed to expend extra time and energy to dig for more information. In the business of daily news reporting, time to dig is rarely forthcoming, so that reporters keep a narrow focus on the obvious principals of the story. Blaming the individual reporter would be to miss the forest for a tree; it is how the media generally operate that led the reporter to construct the story as he did. Functioning within these strict limits is one important mechanism through which the news media, as Richard Ericson and his co-authors have noted, contribute mightily to "the ability of authorities to make convincing claims" (Ericson, Baranek and Chan, 1991: 8). Thus, contrary to appearances, in writing his story on *Peters v. Campbell*, the *Globe and Mail* reporter was not acting as a "Native Affairs Reporter", which is how his by-line often identified him. Rather, on this day he was writing as a legal affairs reporter, and he was only identified as a member of the "British Columbia Bureau". More than any-

---

7 See Canadian Daily Newspaper Publishers Association, "A Statement of Principles for Canadian Daily Newspapers," April 1977; reproduced in Desbarats (1990: 231-2).

thing else, his story was about how the Canadian state, through the Court, was arbitrating conflicts of rights.

"(N)ews of law," Ericson, Baranek and Chan write, "serves as an influential vehicle through which the authority system can instruct people on what to *be* as well as what to *do*" (1991: 7; emphasis in the original). In the story of the initiation of Joseph Peters as told by *The Globe and Mail*, there is no doubt what we the readers should be: we should be like Joseph Peters in his concern for the individual rights of Canadian citizens, and we should be unlike his initiators who put collective rights first. Most importantly, we should be very much unlike a culture that would allow a man to be subjected to such an "ordeal."

We will see below that there were alternatives to this way of telling the story of *Peters v. Campbell*. But, as it is, the newspaper reader is placed in a position where s/he has to choose sides and, given the silences (in terms of cultural context and event-specific motivations) in the story as told, the party to be sided with is us, civilized, modern society, against a primitive, savage practice. This is a morality tale, then, which makes us moderns feel good about ourselves, about our respect for human rights, and which at the same time undermines our ability to respect aboriginal cultures. Most of all it allows us, when we hear the word "Indian" or "aboriginal," to displace concerns, from our domination of them to *their* "savagery." At work here is what Dominick LaCapra calls "the scapegoat mechanism – a mechanism that generates purity for an in-group by projecting all corruption or pollution onto an out-group" (quoted in Krupat 1992: 19).

● ● ●

The last part of the *Peters v. Campbell* story as told by *The Globe and Mail* consists of excerpts from an interview with the defendants' lawyer. These excerpts provide the article with the "balance" called for by the rules of contemporary reporting, in this case outlining an aboriginal cultural and political critique of the judgment. The first excerpt immediately follows the account of the court's decision:

> Native leaders on Vancouver Island greeted the judgement with a great deal of anger, lawyer Lara Skye said yesterday in an interview. "They see it as a complete denial of their constitutionally protected rights."

> Canadian judges, who have been indoctrinated in the Western European tradition of individual rights, have difficulty conceptually in putting collective aboriginal rights in the proper perspective, Ms. Skye said.

This aboriginal narrative is then interrupted by several paragraphs describing the contentious syewen initiation. Then, the article concludes:

> She said in an interview that most ceremonies involve voluntary participants because they consider the ritual to be an honour. But according to tradition, members of a family may request that a relative be initiated involuntarily in order to help with personal problems, such as drinking, drug abuse or other social illnesses.

> The native people do not believe an individual is an island in this world, she said; an individual is part of a family and the family is responsible for the welfare of its members.

Contrary to the reporter's own construction of the suit, which is based on Judge Hood's narration of testimony, Lara Skye places herself[8] and her people outside modernity, and finds it cold and unappealing. She first presents it as oppressive of aboriginal rights specifically. Second, she portrays it as obsessed with the isolated individual and his or her rights, and uncomprehending of collective rights in general.

This broad outline of a critique of whitestream society sounds some familiar complaints about contemporary occidental societies: there is an excess of individualism, the family is in crisis. But whereas whitestream critics of our times target excesses or specific ills of our societies (e.g., individualism is good, but too much of it is bad),[9] this aboriginal critique takes aim at the whole "Western European tradition of individual rights."[10] On the other hand, Skye presents the syewen ritual as an honour, and the native family as caring and nurturing. This echoes the defense's submission to Judge Hood, which he quoted in his decision: "… the primary reason for a Coast Salish family to request that one of their members be initiated is to enhance the quality of the life of the initiate and to honour him" (158).

Problems of the individual that may warrant intervention by the family, says the defense lawyer as quoted in *The Globe and Mail*, are such things as "drinking, drug abuse, and other social illnesses" – problems, by the way,

---

8 She herself is of aboriginal ancestry. At the same time, she, a practising lawyer in British Columbia, lives very much within modernity. Or, perhaps more accurately, modernity lives within her, as it does for all those whose lives it has been shaping. It is hard to imagine that anyone in Canada, as in much of the world, escapes this fate. This raises the question of "hybridity" (see Young, 1995), for clearly modernity and aboriginality are alive in Ms. Skye. We will return to the issue of hybridity in later chapters.

9 In the Canadian context, see for example Reginald Bibby's (1990) quite popular (and conservative) sociological essay *Mosaic Madness*.

10 This indictment, only hinted at in *The Globe and Mail*, is developed much more fully by Turpel (1990).

which are strongly associated with the oppression of aboriginal peoples by whitestream society. Two things are remarkable here: first, whereas the circumstances of the Peters initiation are narrated specifically (this thing happened to this man), the justification for initiating without consent is presented as a general statement, which may or may not apply to this case. Second, the statement of justification comes at the very end of the article, well after reader sympathies have been established and after many readers will have moved on to some other article, for few newspaper articles are read to the end.

Indeed, the standard way to write a newspaper article remains that of the "inverted pyramid," in which the "lead" presents what the reporter / editor considers the most important element of the story, and the remaining elements are presented in descending order of importance. As Carman Cumming and Catherine McKercher note in *The Canadian Reporter* (1994), not only does this model allow an editor to "cut from the bottom" if the article is too long for the space available, but it functions as "an aid to newspaper readers, who can scan and catch the essence of a number of stories, making more or less constant decisions about whether to stay with the story or let their eye slip over to another" (Cumming and McKercher, 1994: 133; see also Larue-Langlois, 1989). In this context, it is significant, to say the least, that the aboriginal rationale for the initiation of Joseph Peters comes at the end of an article that begins with news of a judicial decision.

In reporting as it did, even as it followed accepted rules of "balance," *The Globe and Mail* made itself an auxiliary of the Court, and contributed to the reproduction of the domination of aboriginal cultures by whitestream practices. This is best seen by the reporter's neglect of the initiators' motivations, in conformity with the Court finding them irrelevant. There may be reasons of law that would lead the Court to take this stance (and thereby uphold colonialism), but these are not binding on newspaper reporting and the notion that the initiation without consent was justified by vague marital problems was certainly outlandish enough to raise further questions.

If the article's point had been to make sense of the conflict between Peters and his initiators, further journalistic investigation would have been in order, which would have brought the reporter to consider facts and issues beyond what the Court found relevant. He would have had to look a little more seriously at Coast Salish culture. But he did not, because daily journalism rarely allows such in-depth work. Given this practice, readers are systematically denied access to the unfamiliar, or rather they are given such skewed access that they are bound to recoil from the caricatured other.

In this case, the cultural context within which the initiators acted was badly distorted, and the specific events that led to the initiation were obscured. As a result, the narration of the "two sides" was severely unequal. Readers were presented with those facts of the Peters initiation which the

Court judged relevant, and they were to make sense of those facts either on the basis of the modern cultural context with which they are utterly familiar (as water is familiar to fish), or of an aboriginal context which appeared not even as a cipher but as a blank.

How could this happen? Quite simply, this unequal narration happened because the event being reported was this: the Supreme Court of British Columbia has made a decision, and this decision reaffirms the rule of "English law" over aboriginal practices. In reporting on the Court, the reporter tells the Court's story, which is inherently colonialist (much more on this in Chapter 4). The editorial, coming just a few days later, said explicitly what had been inscribed in the news report's narrative structure. The colonialism of Canada's legal system is, thus, spoken through the media, with its very own moralizing spin on the story.

● ● ●

One of the very peculiar features of the *Peters v. Campbell* decision, as we have already seen, is its account and neglect of the reasons why the initiation of Joseph Peters was carried out without his consent. This, in the end, is the heart of the story I am telling about *Peters v. Campbell*: the fact that the initiators' reasons do not count, and the fact that they should. Although it is clear how Judge Hood's cultural and institutional blindfold would lead him to think these reasons irrelevant, the marginality of the discussion of motivation remains startling. It is almost as though the initiation had been a gratuitous act. Indeed, as processed by the legal system, the initiation is without legitimate motivations, a fact that erases almost any motivation from the story. In narrating testimony, Judge Hood casually refers (1) to "marital and other problems"; (2) to Pat Michaels, whom he quotes as saying that "for us, it was the right thing to do – I thought it would help our relationship"; and (3) to an elder who, on being told by Pat Michaels that Joseph Peters was drinking, replied that they needed "more reason than that" (145-147).

Before going any further, let us consider for a moment these very anemic statements, so as to discount the notion that, through this forced initiation, Joseph Peters was being punished. In the ritual of initiation to syewen, the override of the individual's consent bears an analogy, not to the imprisonment of a criminal, but rather to the "involuntary civil confinement" of a mentally incompetent person which, under the best of assumptions, has a therapeutic rationale.

Described in whitestream terms, syewen clearly aims partly at therapy,[11]

---

11 On this issue, see Amoss (1978), *Coast Salish Spirit Dancing* and Jilek (1974). Anthropological literature has pointed to the "therapeutic" vocation of the trance in other cultural contexts (such as Africa and Brasil) as well; see Bastide (1972). Both Amoss and Jilek indicate that the efficacy of this "therapy" is uneven among the Coast Salish, but the issue of whether or not it

at once psychological and spiritual. Its goal, then, is far better understood as an attempt to heal a wounded spirit than as punishment of a criminal. Further to the point: the theme of healing is a central one in the accounts given by aboriginal people of their attempts to overcome the devastation that has been wrought on their lives by whitestream domination (see for instance Mercredi and Turpel, 1993), and which often expresses itself in alcohol and/or drug addiction, prostitution, suicide, and violence against women – "social illnesses," several of which are also defined as crimes under current whitestream laws.[12] It would therefore be a serious misunderstanding to portray the initiation process as an instance of aboriginal justice, where the initiation ritual would be a trial, conviction, and sentence rolled into one.

I might restate here that my attempt to "think otherwise", while aiming at approaching an aboriginal perspective, remains firmly anchored within an occidental description of the world. I may be able, within my own language, to make some sense of aboriginal ways, but once I have redescribed some of their cultural language to my own, I have not produced one single language, one single description of the world. It is as when I began: there are two cultures, two descriptions of the world, not one. If the issue of cultural redescription is not a problem in and of itself, my attempt at approaching an aboriginal perspective faces an important impediment: I must tease out the motivation of the initiators from the hints and silences of the court's decision and of the various newspaper accounts. Highly intriguing but inconclusive legal files also come into play. The facts to be considered are these:

1. The Court tells us that the initiators had good intentions and that they thought that Joseph Peters needed help.

2. In her *Globe and Mail* interview (GM 1), the defendant's lawyer Lara Skye says that typical reasons for a family to request an initiation, are "alcohol, drugs, and other social illnesses." But at least one elder involved in the decision to initiate Joseph Peters thought alcohol to be insufficient. And we also have Pat Michaels' claim in Court that there were "marital and other problems."

3. *The Regional News* reported that the initiation had been "in atonement for Peters's separation from his wife and children" (RN 2) – a strong suggestion that he was considered singularly at fault. The same article reported an interview with staff sergeant Ray Klaussen of Islandtown's RCMP

---

works is irrelevant here. Besides, although Canada's justice system, like that of other liberal democracies, claims to try to rehabilitate convicted criminals, its actual "redeeming" abilities are, to say the least, limited.

12 Significantly, Bastide writes that in other cultural contexts, one of the "manifest functions" of "possession cults" is to "reconstitute solidarities damaged by changes in social structure, and in particular family solidarities" (Bastide, 1972: 85; my translation). For Bastide's distinction between trance and possession, see Chapter 6, note 25.

Detachment.[13] Klaussen claimed that Peters had arranged a meeting with police several days before going public with his story, but failed to keep the appointment; the RCMP never received an official request from Peters to investigate the incident, and that may have led to criminal charges. Klaussen was further quoted as saying, "Peters knows the ins and outs of the law. Either he should launch an investigation or keep his mouth shut." This seems a remarkably unsympathetic statement towards a person who was to be considered a victim by the BC Supreme Court.

4. My curiosity spurred by staff sergeant Klaussen's hint of Peters's familiarity with "the law," I inquired at Islandtown's Court Registry about his possible presence in other court cases. I first received a warning about the possible confidentiality of such information, but they were able to tell me, as part of "the public record," that Peters had indeed been arrested and criminally charged, in February 1992, with possession of narcotics for the purpose of trafficking, and that the charge was dismissed in June 1993. (This arrest came four years after his initiation, and days after he won his lawsuit.) For further information, I was directed to speak with Islandtown's federal crown prosecutor. He, in turn, warned that he may not be able to reveal information, and that he would have to seek direction from the federal crown's provincial head office in Vancouver. This done, here is what he was able to tell me, again as a matter of "public record" taken from his files: Peters had been arrested for a routine traffic violation at the wheel of his brother's car with his brother sitting beside him; the police found a sportsbag containing narcotics in the back of the car. At trial, Peters claimed that he had stepped into the car only minutes before the arrest, that the bag was already there, and that he was not aware of its presence, much less of its contents. The trial judge found that there was reasonable doubt, and therefore acquitted him.

We remain uncertain as to what actually took place that led to the initiation, including the specific nature of the "marital and other problems" that moved Pat Michaels to request a forced initiation. (And remember that the drug charge, of which he was acquitted, occurred four years *after* the initiation.)[14]

---

13 In British Columbia, the Royal Canadian Mounted Police (RCMP) provides municipal police services outside large cities.

14 This has called on me to make an extremely difficult decision: should I include this incident in my story, or leave it out on the basis that Peters was acquitted and that, in any case, his arrest and trial happened much later than the events surrounding the initiation? I chose to include the incident because my knowledge of it would have been somehow present in the book as a kind of hovering ghost, perhaps producing an impression of something held back. By including it, I invite readers to conduct their own evaluation of what, if anything, it amounts to, and of the necessary decisions involved in constructing a narrrative.

Whatever the specific issue, or "social illness" in the words of Lara Skye, it is clear that (A) Pat Michaels thought that her problems with her partner were sufficiently serious that she needed the help of the community and that he bore enough responsibility for them that he should be initiated whether or not he agreed to it; and (B) the elders needed what they thought of as good and compelling reasons to carry out an initiation without the consent of the initiate. And, as we will see, there is nothing arbitrary about the way in which the elders made their decision. Thus, if we are to take seriously and respect aboriginal cultures, we should be prepared to defer to their decision-making process and to the decisions themselves. (This is, of course, what Canadian courts are generally not prepared to do.) In other words, we should be prepared to assume that aboriginal people would not engage in the gratuitous, disproportionate or wanton infliction of pain and suffering, the contrary assumption being nothing short of racist.

Clearly, however, things can go wrong during an initiation, whether it is coerced or not. Thus, *The Regional News* reported that, just before Joseph Peters's initiation, another man died during his own initiation (RN 1). He was the third person in Islandtown to die in this way, and the seventh in BC since 1972, all deaths which were the object of a coroner's investigation (RN 3). Asked about the deaths and the initiations themselves by the *Regional News* reporter, the coroner responded that the deaths had been linked "with everything from alcohol withdrawal to excessive beatings." He then added: "It's a ceremony that's protected by the Charter of Rights... And regardless of the controversy over the deaths related to alcohol withdrawal, the natives had a better track record of rehabilitating their people than we have"[15] (RN 3).

Things can also go wrong in a less tragic way, as did happen during Joseph Peters's initiation. At the beginning of the initiation, he had been asked by the men in charge of the ritual whether he had any health problem about which they should know and that they should monitor; he responded that he had a peptic ulcer. During the fourth day, he complained that his ulcer was flaring up. His initiators let him leave and he immediately went to the hospital, where a physician took care of what he described at trial as a minor condition. There is no question that a four-day fast is a severe drain on the body's resources, and that a variety of organs can cease functioning quite properly. If a person is in ill-health to begin with, or is alcohol- or drug-dependent, the fast can have tragic consequences even if the initiation is conducted in the most careful way, and the initiate's condition is monitored by Longhouse elders. This shows two things: first, as the ritual proceeds, the initiators will concern themselves for the initiate's well-being; second, among First Nations as within whitestream society, accidents happen.

---

15 The *Peters v. Campbell* decision, of course, put a serious damper on the coroner's claim that syewen is protected by the Charter. Judge Hood found that consensual syewen initiations may be protected, but that coerced initiations certainly were not.

What about the question, that may come easily to whitestream sensibilities, that due process was denied Joseph Peters? What we call due process is a culturally specific practice, and the circumstances that led to the initiation may be said to represent a Coast Salish version of due process. The initiation would not be undertaken without consent, unless the elders in charge of the ritual were satisfied that there were good reasons to do so, as guaranteed by at least one member of the prospective initiate's family. In such a situation, due process is not dependent on a court of law and the adversarial system, but on the trust that a community puts in certain men and women, endowing them with the status of elder. Thus, both in substantive terms and in procedural terms, an initiation without consent is not an arbitrarily conducted event.

In the case of the initiation of Joseph Peters, his lack of consent may have been the truly irrelevant issue. Whether or not it in fact was irrelevant is not a question which need detain us here. The point is that the eventual irrelevance of Joseph Peters's lack of consent could not be established by a Canadian court. A conceptual category such as "wounded spirit" (upon which the legitimacy of a coerced initiation turns) is not one that can be handled by such a court – only an aboriginal process could deal with it. Assuming a process of aboriginal justice, some kind of recourse would undoubtedly have been available to Joseph Peters that could establish whether or not his initiation had been gratuitous and unjustified according to aboriginal criteria of justice. Only a Coast Salish process could do this.[16]

I have already noted that, within the whitestream description of the world, there are circumstances where the suspension of individual rights is deemed legitimate, and this suspension may extend to the infliction of pain and suffering. Thus, convicted criminals are deprived of certain rights as are some people who are judged mentally incompetent to take care of themselves, and who may be subjected, for instance, to electroshock treatments without their consent being a factor in the decision. Presumably, the Coast Salish description of the world also allows for such overrides of individual autonomy. This should not surprise moderns, schooled in the myth that we are unique in our concern and respect for individual freedom. What we can see from the initiation of Joseph Peters shows, however, that there is a large amount of respect in Coast Salish culture for individual autonomy.

Judge Hood's narration of the events leading to the initiation includes this sequence:[17] when Pat Michaels went to see the elders, asking for Peters to be initiated, they were reluctant to agree to her request. Not only did

---

16 More on such a process in Chapter 4. On aboriginal conceptions of governance, see also Canada (1996B).

17 The sequence played no part in Judge Hood's decision, for he considered the process followed by the elders, as well as their motivation of course, to be irrelevant.

they ask her to make her case, but they insisted that another member of his family confirm the request; only when she came back with the permission of Joseph Peters's brother did the elders decide to go ahead with the initiation.[18] Three steps, then, had to be followed: initiation ceremonies will be undertaken without the consent of the initiate only in such cases where a request is made by a member of the initate-to-be's family, where there are good and compelling reasons, and after due consideration of whether or not it should go ahead.

This kind of concern is consistent with research showing a strong individualist streak in Coast Salish culture (Amoss, 1978) and others such as the Dene (Guédon, 1994). Clearly, the Coast Salish and whitestream cultures have different ways of making decisions and of disregarding individual autonomy. But there obviously are situations where both cultures identify the same social practice as unacceptable and subject to some community action upon the individual. Think, by way of example, of something that does not apply in this case: murder. The purposeful killing of a member by another is not accepted by either culture, except in special circumstances, for instance, legitimate defence, which removes from the killing the label "murder."

It could be, then, that if Pat Michaels had chosen to go to the whitestream community with her claims to needing help for herself and her husband, she would have obtained "our" version of help; or perhaps not, depending on the specifics of her story, which may or may not have been more compelling for one culture than for the other. But she chose to appeal to the Coast Salish community, and to bring into play aboriginal cultural practices. The Coast Salish community responded to her appeal, and was later told by the BC Supreme Court that it had no right to do so in the way it did.

● ● ●

This, then, is not a conflict between valuing individual or collective rights contrary to the standard accounts of the cultural difference between the occidental and aboriginal worlds, including the comments of lawyer Lara Skye published in *The Globe and Mail*. Indeed, some features of syewen make it very clear that a strong individualist streak exists in Coast Salish culture as is argued, it turns out, in the book that the defendants submitted to the court as a "learned treatise" whose facts should be treated as *prima facie* true (154).[19] Which is not to say, of course, that the Coast Salish people see the individual as an island, isolated from family and community.

---

18 We will see in later chapters that there are complications in this sequence.

19 The book is Amoss (1978).

As I understand it, the relationship between individualism and collectivism in Coast Salish culture is dialectical: they feed on each other, in a state of tension as much as of reinforcement. Now this is also the case in occidental culture, at least as individualism is constructed in philosophical and ethical systems. This dialectic of individual, family and community is, for instance, at the heart of hellenistic individualism (see Foucault, 1984B). It is also crucial in the genesis of modern individualism.[20] Thus, as Anthony Giddens has argued, "autonomy is not the same as egoism and moreover implies reciprocity and interdependence" (Giddens, 1994: 13).

There are, then, some things that are shared by the aboriginal and occidental perspectives, "meta-cultural" features perhaps, but which are constructed and expressed in ways specific to each. Because of this phenomenological depth, the simple "two sides" structure – us and them, irreconcilably opposed – of the newspaper report, and of lawyer Lara Skye's comments, is deeply misleading. More importantly, it induces readers, the audience, to take the dominant's side on the basis of a binary opposition that need not exist, but that covers the weak's side with a veil of ignorance.[21]

At a seminar in which I presented some elements of the *Peters v. Campbell* story, I was asked a question for which I was not prepared. I had thought about the issue several months before, but had not returned to it since then, and could not offer a decent answer. I had just argued, first, that surely every culture on the planet has some kind of respect for individual autonomy, given certain community constraints on individual actions, and that this is the case anyway with the Coast Salish process of coerced syewen initiation. And, second, that outsiders such as myself ought to sufficiently respect the Coast Salish people to defer to their decision-making, even, and especially, when we might be tempted to spontaneously disapprove of its outcome. (Deference, I should add, does not preclude trying to make sense of, to redescribe, an apparently alien practice, to the point perhaps of coming to agree with it.) The question was this: what does this stance of respect and deference have to say about practices such as female genital mutilation in a number of African countries? Wasn't my *Peters v. Campbell* case conveniently avoiding difficult issues raised more explicitly by that other situation?

I was, to a large extent, stumped. Accepting the validity of the analogy between the two situations, I replied something to this effect: no matter how much I disapprove of a particular practice, or of a whole set of practices, that disapproval does not give me the right to rule over the people concerned, whether one is dealing with an inter-state situation or a within-

---

20 Among a multitude of discussions of this issue, see Taylor (1989, 1991).

21 Readers of John Rawls (1972) will be familiar with this phrase, of course. But I am using it in a sharply different sense, referring to the invisibility of the oppressed. This is a veil of ignorance that is all too present in social life, as opposed to Rawls's theoretical justice-producing tool.

state situation in which a group's right to self-government is recognized. I may try to convince them to stop, I may encourage my government to engage in a variety of sanctions against the country that allows the practice, but I cannot, through greater force, decide for them and enforce my decision against their will. I would add here that there is a point at which sanctions become an instrument of overwhelming force, when the parties are of very unequal strength; in such a case, the presumed wrong at which the sanctions are aimed would have to be similarly overwhelming for the sanctions to be justified, if at all.

This response still strikes me as correct, as far as it goes. But it does not go far enough, because the validity of the analogy has to be challenged. As a good liberal, I was lulled into accepting it because coerced initiation and genital mutilation both treat the individual's consent as irrelevant and involve the infliction of physical injury which are, of course, liberalism's cardinal sins. But there is a controlling difference between the two cases: it is that an initiation such as Joseph Peters's is the outcome of an individual decision flowing from specific circumstances and in which a specific person is thought to need help. Further (but this is secondary), the injurious action is specifically and directly aimed at enhancing the initiate's spiritual well-being, and the injuries are not long-lasting, whereas genital mutilation is a blanket means of disciplining a whole subordinated category of the population.

The two cases, then, could hardly be further apart. Indeed, the initiation of Joseph Peters is very much an instance of a community that respects individual autonomy at the same time that it feels the need to exercise a degree of control over its members, a pattern entirely consistent with whitestream conceptions of human rights, in a way that female genital mutilation is not.

Still, for many, perhaps most, readers, there will remain something hard to swallow about the experience of Joseph Peters. His story is certainly enough for us to conclude that there is nothing meek about the initiation to syewen. Add to this that the physical trauma of the initiation is sometimes (rarely) sufficient to cause death, and chances are that when whitestream Canadians read about such things, they are going to be outraged. But what is it, specifically, that offends? What are these readers doing in the process of being outraged? They are passing moral judgement on the actions of the initiators.

A basic way to describe what makes something "moral" is to say that (A) a particular social rule applies to everyone in a community and that (B) there is a good reason for this rule to exist: it is thought to be justified rather than arbitrary (see Narveson, 1993). More substantively, it could be said, following Charles Taylor, that morality accounts for a large portion of the domain of "strong evaluation": "Perhaps the most urgent and powerful cluster of demands that we recognize as moral concern the respect for the life, integrity, and well-being, even flourishing, of others" (Taylor, 1989: 4).

In this case, in Western societies there are clearly rules applying to everyone against confining people against their will, starving and beating them. These rules are key elements of what makes these societies liberal and modern. Two such rules are crucial for our purposes. The first one may be said to belong to the realm of political morality and applies to modern societies, whether or not they are liberal: the only legitimate violence is that which is state-authorized. Individuals acting on their own behalf cannot forcibly take someone in their custody, much less beat and starve them. The second rule is more general (in the sense that it constrains not only private agents but also state-authorized agents), and is intimately connected to what makes certain modern societies liberal. It holds that cruelty is wrong, and that as such it ought to be avoided by everyone, including and in particular those acting on behalf of the state.

Liberals have defined cruelty as "the deliberate infliction of physical, and secondarily emotional, pain upon a weaker person or group by stronger ones in order to achieve some end, tangible or intangible, of the latter" (Shklar, 1989: 29). The beating and starving of prisoners legitimately held by the state is illegitimate, both as punishment and as pressure tactics for such things as obtaining confessions or denunciations.[22] Liberalism, in turn, "is a political theory of limited government, providing for personal liberty," such that it is opposed to "political absolutism and arbitrariness, and an array of officially sanctioned obstacles to the free exercise of religion, speech, and association" (Rosenblum, 1989: 5).

We live within liberal modernity,[23] then, in that we severely limit the things that (agents of) our governments can do to individuals. Most of all we do not allow cruelty: "liberalism's deepest grounding is in place from the first, in the conviction of the earliest defenders of toleration, born in horror, that cruelty is an absolute evil, an offense against God or humanity" (Shklar, 1989: 23. See also Rorty, 1989).[24] The 8th Amendment to the American Constitution is a milestone in this respect, prohibiting cruel and unusual punishment. It followed in the footsteps of the English Bill of Rights of 1689,[25] and was itself followed two hundred years later by the Canadian

---

22 Although police brutality for the latter purpose is often taken for granted, if not explicitly condoned by our society's polite majorities.

23 There is, then, clearly no redundance in speaking of "liberal modernity": while, for instance, soviet-type state socialism was clearly modern, it was obviously illiberal. Any number of twentieth century dictatorships would also fit the bill of illiberal modernity, as would even more nineteenth century political regimes (see Shklar, 1989).

24 More on the historical context in which liberalism arose, in Chapter 6.

25 The 8th Amendment also prohibits the setting of excessive bail or the imposition of excessive fines. The whole amendment is "taken almost verbatim from the English Bill of Rights of 1689, which provides that "excessive bail ought not to be required, nor excessive fines imposed, nor cruel and unusual punishments inflicted." (*New Multimedia Encyclopedia* [Grolier Electronic Publishing, 1993], article "Eight Amendment.").

Charter of Rights and Freedoms: "Everyone has the right not to be subjected to any cruel and unusual treatment or punishment" (Article 12).

As Charles Taylor would have it, "we are *much more* sensitive on this score than our ancestors of a few centuries ago" (Taylor, 1989: 12; emphasis added). On liberalism's definition, what was done to Joseph Peters could easily be conceived as cruel, and this is certainly how the editorial writer at *The Globe and Mail* saw it, and how most its readers are likely to see it. But we run here against the evolutionist element in liberal thinking, which should give us pause. The history of punishment in Western societies is one that is usually told as involving progress, with the development of humane penalties (i.e. prison) by modernity, as opposed to the inhumane and cruel, indeed savage or barbaric, pre-modern penalties of "our ancestors," pre-modern Europeans, in Taylor's phrase, but also First Nations according to evolutionist ideas about "primitive" societies as representing "our" past. This evolutionist account has been famously challenged by Michel Foucault (1975): what is at stake is not more or less cruelty, more or less sensitivity to suffering, but differing standards and strategies for allocating deviance, in the context of particular technologies of administration and social power, inducing and feeding upon different conceptions of cruelty and suffering.[26]

Some of Foucault's anti-evolutionist claim is almost accepted by Taylor when he invites us to "consider the (to us) *barbarous* punishments" our ancestors inflicted on criminals (Taylor, 1989: 12; emphasis added). His bracketed "to us" is an admission that barbarity is in the eye of the beholder. From there it is a short step to conclude that what counts as sensitivity to suffering will vary from one context to another. We are sensitive to different things than what struck our ancestors as deserving of sensitivity. But this is a step which Taylor refuses to take. The "terrible punishment" meted out in the pre-modern world, he writes, was called for as the corresponding ritual undoing of a terrible crime, in the context of a worldview that saw "human beings as playing a role in a larger cosmic order or divine history"; secular modernity has done away with "the needless, senseless suffering inflicted on humans in the name of such large orders or dramas" (Taylor, 1989: 13).

The notion of the "ordeal" as a primitive judicial process belongs to the same frame of mind. Moderns would think the ordeal primitive because of its cruelty and its religious underpinnings. This outlook, down to Taylor's use of the category "barbarous," remains very much inscribed in Enlightenment rationalism which, as Robert Young (1995) argues, is founded on the simultaneous discursive creation of "savagery" and "bar-

---

26 Which is not to say that punishment has ceased targeting the body, for imprisonment also involves forms of physical suffering. Asks Foucault, "What could non-corporal punishment be?" (Foucault, 1975: 21).

barism" in a three-stages model of human history. Civilization is defined "through difference, against a hierarchy that invokes the state of other, historical or non-European, societies. Liberalism itself has relied on this model, first formalized by J.S. Mill in his essay "Civilization," which formulated "the trio ... as a hierarchy of the historical stages of man, bringing geography and history together in a generalized scheme of European superiority that identified civilization with race" (Young, 1995: 35). And, however much other societies are denigrated in schemes such as Mill's, by "being placed lower on the scale, (they) were by the same token nevertheless essential to the European sense of self and concept of civilization" (Young, 1995: 35; see also, classically, Said, 1978).

That this inherently racist scheme is a pillar of the thought of Mill, one of the patron saints of liberalism, exposes the deep flaw in Stephen Holmes's (1989) arguments about "the permanent structure of antiliberal thought." Holmes has a field day showing thematic connections between nineteenth century reactionaries, early twentieth century fascists, and contemporary "antiliberal" authors.[27] But, as Young (1995) shows, the influence of racialist theory was so endemic in nineteenth century science that no intellectual practice today can claim an unblemished pedigree.

The question is: how is one related today to such antecedents as one has? If one considers that discourse is always in situation, it is clear that similar words have the capacity to function differently in different contexts. While often rhetorically effective, it is therefore dishonest for liberals (and others) to insinuate some automatic sinister connection between a discredited politics of the past and contemporary intellectual currents that are best characterized as progressive. It is not clear, on the other hand, that liberalism has disentangled itself from racist premises, as the unreflexive centrality of "cruelty" and the continued relevance of the barbarous / civilized opposition in Taylor's work indicate. You can only think of yourself as civilized, Taylor writes, if there is somebody else whom you can consider savage or barbarian and who is less sensitive to cruelty than you are.

It is only in retrospect, from our modern vantage point, that the terrible suffering condemned by Taylor can be seen as "needless, senseless." But to our ancestors (whoever they were), these punishments were far from senseless; in Taylor's own account, they made perfect sense in "a cosmic order or divine history." Further, the common modern assumption that "Indians" are cruel – this can be seen in such recent and supposedly correct films as *Dances With Wolves*, *Black Robe* and *The Last of the Mohicans* – is very much a whitestream cultural construct. Georges Sioui, in *For an Amerindian*

---

27 Holmes takes explicit aim at Alisdair MacIntyre, Michael Sandel and Roberto Unger. But other targets are hinted at by his identification of Nietzsche as a touchstone: Michel Foucault and poststructuralist theory come to mind. Holmes has later expanded the argument in a book; see Holmes (1993).

Autohistory (1992), writes that the torture inflicted on prisoners by a number of aboriginal peoples expressed the respect that captors had for the courage of those they had captured; to talk of cruelty in such a situation is a grave misunderstanding. As hard as it may be for moderns to credit this notion of torture as expression of respect, it points to the fundamental problem of overlaying one culture's concepts (such as what the liberal white stream understands as "cruelty") upon another culture.

Liberal philosophers' claim that modernity has left cruelty behind is also undermined by an obvious fact: it is far from clear that various degrees of physical punishment are considered outrageous by a good number of people in contemporary societies considered "liberal." Thus, in Canada and the United States, public opinion has remained consistently in favour of capital punishment – in Canada despite the political class's majority disapproval, which has banned executions since 1976.[28] Also, the 1994 "caning" of American student Michael Faye in Singapore aroused a significant degree of support, in several parts of North America for that kind of punishment. Indeed, in the winter of 1995, the Reform Party's law-enforcement critic in Canada's House of Commons formed the project of visiting Singapore "to study his pet idea of flogging sex offenders" (Mason Lee, 1996: D2).

It turns out, then, that "we" in modern liberal societies are not all liberals, and that what some consider a cruel punishment is thought perfectly all right by others. It becomes necessary to consider the fact that "cruelty" means different things to different cultures and even to different people in the same society, and to put aside Taylor's portrayal, which amounts to a ranking of cultures on an evolutionary scale. Indeed, he writes of the modern West as "unique among higher civilizations" because of "the importance we put on avoiding suffering" (Taylor, 1989: 12).

● ● ●

We should not take modernity at its word when it claims that it is uniquely concerned about human rights and the avoidance of cruelty. This is its own self-glorifying narrative, built on a denigration of others. This brings me to a final discussion of the claim that, while whitestream society is concerned with individual rights, aboriginal societies are all about community. I have tried to show in my analysis of *Peters v. Campbell* that the elders of the syewen tradition had shown considerable respect for Joseph Peters's life, integrity, and well-being. If we go back to Shklar's definition of cruelty, it is clear that the initiators were more powerful than Joseph Peters, and that they were pursuing their own ends of social control; but can it be said confidently that, by wanting to help him, they were not pursuing his own ends

---

28 The last execution in Canada was carried out in 1962. See Carrigan (1991).

as well? And what about the ends of his wife, who requested the initiation and who likely was individually less powerful than he was? In any case, how can the elders' uncontested concern for Peters's welfare be squared with the "community only" view of aboriginal values?

The first thing to do is to be attentive to the political and ideological purchase of statements on individual vs collective rights. We have to read past the obvious political sense of such statements to see the articulation of the relationship between individuals and community. I want to approach this issue through a very helpful statement by Joan Crow, an aboriginal woman trained as (among other things) a lawyer, writing in the feminist paper *Kinesis* about the Canadian Constitution and Charter of Rights[29]:

> The Charter I learned about in white law school is about individual rights. My rights as an individual. That is not how I and many of my people look at ourselves. [We have] another process, a different process ...
>
> Fundamentally, people who espouse these individual values do not accept that we are inherently *connected* to each other. We must first recognize that we are connected. Then our place as an individual is ensured. Because if I'm connected to you and I don't treat you right, you will hold me accountable. If you don't treat me right, I can look you right in the eye and say: "What's going on?" Because we're connected. That's what is called collective rights. (Crow, 1992: 7. Emphasis in the original)

Beyond her proclaimed hostility to "individual rights" and her affirmation of "collective rights," Crow is telling a story of how, in her world, a person is entitled to be treated with respect by others at the same time that she has a responsibility to treat others with respect. An individual who deviates from what is considered respectful behaviour toward another individual or the community as a whole, will be called to account. This is entirely consistent with whitestream conceptions of deviance. It is from this recognition of connectedness that "our place as an individual is ensured." The same point is made, with some extra emphasis, by a Coast Salish elder in reaction to Joseph Peters's lawsuit. Perhaps it should be expected that, seeing his community's traditions challenged in the name of "individual rights," he would respond with scorn for the concept that is being used as a weapon against him :

---

29 See also Mercredi and Turpel (1993: 96-106).

In our culture those kinds of rights, as you call them, aren't applicable
... One may be 19 years of age ... you could be married and have children of your own, and your parents would still impose discipline on
you in how you should live. In our culture, despite who or what you
are, you are still subject to the discipline of our people (RN 6).

As was the case with Lara Skye's comments, the expression "individual
rights" is assimilated to the isolation of the person, to her dis-connectedness,
and to the ensuing lack of respect of individuals for one another. The aboriginal outlook, on the other hand, emphasizes connectedness and respect
for the person. In contemporary Canadian politics, unfortunately, this is a
message of re-definition that is not likely to be heard because of the hegemonic understanding and spontaneous commitment to "individual rights".
What will tend to be heard is the repudiation of individual rights in favour
of collective rights, a tendency that will be reinforced by modernity's self-
glorification as uniquely respectful of individual rights.

What of that self-glorification, though? On the respect for the life,
integrity and well-being of others, that are "the most urgent and powerful"
of moral concerns, Taylor writes: "Virtually everyone feels these demands,
and they have been and are acknowledged *in all human societies* ... We are
dealing here with moral intuitions which are uncommonly deep, powerful,
and *universal*" (Taylor, 1989: 4; emphasis added). We have seen it at work
among the Coast Salish elders. There is nothing particular to modernity
here, then. But modernity's "favoured formulation for this principle of
respect has come to be in terms of rights" (Taylor, 1989: 11). It is important
to look past this "formulation" to other descriptions that may allow a bridge
between cultures. Thus, if the label "rights" is a unique formulation, the
respect for autonomy that rights express may be recognizably present in
other cultures.

It would be a grave mistake, in this perspective, to think that there is
nothing behind the rights formulation of respect, a mistake made, I am
afraid, by those who say that the Western conception of rights is fundamentally alien to aboriginal conceptions because rights are based on private
property, which is foreign to First Nations (see, for instance, Turpel, 1990).
The fact is that private property is something that attaches to individuals, and
it is because the individuals' autonomy is respected that rights are tied to
their property (that some individuals have more property than others is why
the former feel a need to protect it). The Western concept of rights, then,
is foreign to First Nations in that it is a specific language which has developed in specific historical circumstances. But it is not fundamentally foreign:
structural features relating to respect for individual autonomy are shared.

What is peculiar to modernity, writes Taylor, is this: "Modern culture
has developed conceptions of individualism which picture the human per-

son as ... declaring independence from the webs of interlocution which have originally formed him/her, or at least neutralizing them" (Taylor, 1989: 36). Although "one cannot be a self on one's own" (Taylor, 1989: 36), modernity strives for that dis-connectedness, indeed for the individual to be able to stand against the community, a model of this stance being Socrates as portrayed by Plato as "able to stand in imperious independence of Athenian *opinion*." (Taylor, 37; emphasis added) But Socrates was not able to stand in any kind of independence of Athenian *society*. One may hold a view of such narcissist isolation, but will not live that life (except for the very few hermits whom we find scattered throughout human history).

What is particular to modernity, then, is not a respect for individual life, integrity, and well-being, which in various ways is surely universal, but rather a hypertrophied regard for the independent self, a self that in any case is never lived, for this independence is not possible. The independent self is merely ideologized. We will see below that this hypertrophy[30] is related to the modern banishment of the spiritual from the public realm, a displacement lastingly captured in Nietzsche's quip that "God is dead." But in *The Gay Science*'s paragraph just above this famous one, those who would sever connections are warned:

> We have left the land and we have embarked! ... Well! Little boat, beware! The ocean lies next to you: it is true that it does not always roar, and sometimes its surface rests as silk and gold, a daydream of goodness. But there will be times when you will realize that it is infinite and that there is nothing so terrible as infinity. Alas! poor bird, once you thought yourself free, but now you come up against this cage's bars! Woe upon you, if you grow homesick, as if there was more *freedom* back there, – and now, "land" is no longer. (Nietzsche, *The Gay Science*, §124)[31]

● ● ●

In modernity, the individual self is ideologically sovereign and to become so, it must sever ties to the community and kill God. The cultural project of aboriginality is critical of modernity on both counts: it calls for the re-insertion of the individual in the community and a return of the community to spirituality. Materially, of course, modern individuals never do leave the community, and aboriginal concern for the community was never neglectful, much less contemptuous, of the care for individual autonomy.

---

30 This theme of modernity as hypertrophy is developed (and critiqued) by Taylor in a 1985 text, "Alternative Futures: Legitimacy, Identity, and Alienation in Late-Twentieth-Century Canada," reproduced in Taylor (1993).

31 This is my translation, from the French. See Nietzsche (1993A: 131).

It is important, in this context, that the common ground be recognized, both by whitestream Canadians and by members of the First Nations. But most of all, it is primarily whitestream Canadians who have things to learn: first, that political rhetoric and racist conceptions of self / other should be put aside, so as to recognize that aboriginal peoples are quite adept at respecting the life, integrity, and well-being of individuals; and second, that it is not necessarily a good thing to fantasize our selves as dwelling in splendid isolation from family and community.

This latter lesson, in fact, feeds right into one of modernity's own tensions, for alongside the fantasy of the sovereign individual stands an "affirmation of ordinary life," a phrase, writes Taylor (again), that designates "the life of production and the family." (Taylor, 1989: 13) I have already discussed, in the context of Lara Skye's comments, the currently fashionable complaint among moderns about the excess of individualism and the need to re-emphasize family and community.

The affirmation of ordinary life is supposed to be a trait specific to modernity, in contradistinction in particular to the value that Greek antiquity and Europe's feudal order placed upon the "public" life. Once again, however, this is too narrow a focus, which makes too much of modernity's (claimed) unique virtues. One need only look at Zen's "emphasis on living the ordinary life, which is in accord with the [Taoist] teachings of Lao-tzù and Chuang-tzu," an emphasis that contributed to protecting Zen Buddhism from persecution by the Chinese Emperor Wu in the ninth century (Wu, 1996: 71, 84). The focus is too narrow also in that it neglects Greco-Roman Antiquity's ethic of "the care of the self". In the first and second centuries AD – not a liberal era in any way – there developed philosophies of

> an art of existence gravitating around the question of self, of its dependence and independence, of its universal form and of the tie it can and must develop with others, of the procedures through which it exercises self-control and of the manner in which it can establish its full sovereignty on itself. (Foucault, 1984: 273; my translation)

It would seem, then, that on our cultural map of respect for individual autonomy, three zones can be identified: first, the universally shared respect for life, integrity and well-being, along with a concern for the tension between connectedness and autonomy; second, modernity's hypertrophy of the self's independence; and third, within modernity, a further hypertrophy of the self at the end of the twentieth century. It is this final hypertrophy that is triggering calls, from within modernity itself and from aboriginality, for a certain retrenchment towards connectedness, for limiting modernity's excesses or (if Taylor is right) rescuing its values from "the distortions and perversions that have developed in modern history" (Taylor, 1993: 63).

Chapter 4
Self-government

←——→

I grew up near Canada
Close to Port Alberni
On Vancouver Island
Close to British Columbia
RON HAMILTON
(KI-KE-IN)[1]

From the point of view of the Coast Salish community,[2] what went wrong in the initiation of Joseph Peters? First, and most evidently, their right to deal with problems in their own way and on their own was denied by the Canadian state. But this is merely the end of the line in the community's destructuring, its disarticulation. How so? Someone, Joseph Peters, whom they claim as a member of their community, took the situation out of their hands and brought it to a Canadian court.

The root of the problem is that the Salish community lives in the interstices of a larger society that does not respect it and does not recognize its authority to rule itself. This made it possible for Joseph Peters to get materially out of the community and into one that would shield him from Coast Salish efforts to "heal" him. Suppose that the only option open to Peters in getting out of his initial community had been to land in one that returned him to his starting point: his individual attempt to subvert his community's social controls would have been thwarted, and the community's ability to self-govern would have been confirmed. As it is, the Canadian state's legally inscribed contempt for aboriginal autonomy produces a set of individual options that are destructuring of the Salish community. Peters was able to challenge the community's self-rule by going to an outside, more powerful authority.

The *Peters v. Campbell* case is not likely to be an important one in terms of judicial precedent, but it is extremely revealing of how Canadian courts are wont to think about aboriginal rights. It also allows, despite itself, for a glimpse of just how destructive "our" judicial process is of aboriginal ways of life and of thinking. And it raises important and difficult issues about the future of the relationship for, as in the case of freedom of speech, it becomes

---

1   Ki-ke-in (Ron Hamilton), from "A Part Apart," in Jensen and Brooks (1993: 80).

2   We will look at Peters's point of view in Chapter 6.

really difficult, and important, to respect and defend someone's freedom when we disagree with what they do with it.

In its editorial on the *Peters v. Campbell* decision, *The Globe and Mail* wrote that the case provides a very rare "legal landmark" to think about the concept of a separate aboriginal justice system, discussion of which is too often mired in generalities: "Fundamental justice is not divisible. The law ... should not permit (Mr. Peters's) band to treat him as it did ... Obviously, beyond the attractive generalities of native self-government lie very important specific questions of right and wrong" (GM 2).[3] With this editorial and its previous news report (GM 1), *The Globe and Mail* was making the *Peters v. Campbell* case into a component of the national discussion on the Canada / First Nations relationship. This, to my mind, is an entirely good idea, but it was also using the case to delegitimize aboriginal practices under the guise of affirming "fundamental justice" – and this is entirely problematic. The editorial writer, here, showed no inclination whatsoever to use the case to reflect about our own ideas and practices, and ask herself (or himself) "very important specific questions of right and wrong": it was enough to question the aboriginal practices.

In current political debates about Canadian unity, it is indeed in this context that the issue of collective right is generally brought up: with regard to Quebec and aboriginal peoples, and never on the issue of the collective right of the Canadian state to rule over its (sic) people(s), that is already established. This latter collective right is taken for granted, allowing the Canadian state and those who identify with it to be ostensibly interested only in individual rights, the fully civilized thing to do, while an excessive interest in collective rights can be ascribed to primitive, tribal propensities. But looking at these three collectivities – Canada, Quebec, First Nations – it is easy to find that all three respect the autonomy of the individual while imposing certain limits upon it.

In fact, it is meaningless to oppose individual to collective rights. This has been well noted by Ovide Mercredi, in speaking of his hope that constitutional reform would recognize the inherent right to aboriginal self-government:

> We thought that constitutional reform would allow us to enjoy basic rights that Canadian people take for granted but do not extend to us. Canadian people know the importance of collective rights, of democracy. We have collective rights too, but they are not recognized or fully accepted by the laws of this country. (Mercredi and Turpel, 1993: 86)

---

3   Note the error of fact, which raises an issue to which we will return in Chapter 6: it is not "the band" that initiated Joseph Peters, but rather members of the Longhouse.

Discussion of collective rights, then, should be framed on the basis of the following questions, which were indeed raised by the defendants' lawyer in the Joseph Peters suit: is a given people – say, First Nations, or Quebec – to have jurisdiction over its own collective life and the lives of its individual members, and if so to what extent? Is it, in other words, to self-govern? Or is this authority to be exercised by some larger unit – say, the Canadian state – regardless of the specific ways and desires of the smaller (less powerful) collectivity?

● ● ●

"For natives, the system shoots first and asks questions later," writes Ralph Akiwenzie,[4] Chief of an Ojibway band that lives on Ontario's Bruce Peninsula between Georgian Bay and Lake Huron. That bay, incidentally, was named after the English King George IV; "Huron" is an archaic French word that refers to a hirsute hairstyle or to an ill-mannered person, a "ruffian," and was used as a nickname by French colonists to speak of the members of the aboriginal Wendat confederacy.[5]

The words of our everyday language still do carry colonial and derogatory content; one might ask in what ways this is "Canadian content". Nowhere in Canada is this more evident than in British Columbia, a territory which was made a British colony between 1849 and 1858.[6] Europeans first called their capital Camosun, the Salish name of the rapids in a local gorge, but they later changed their mind and called it Victoria (Hill-Tout, 1978: 128). Victoria's daily newspaper is, unselfconsciously, the *Times-Colonist*. And in Victoria today, there is a Trutch Avenue, named after the province's first lieutenant-governor, who in 1871 decided that "all Indian lands and resources were 'public' lands which were 'automatically' under the control" of Canada's new province (Sewid-Smith, 1993: 28). At that time, the aboriginal population of the province outnumbered Europeans by three to one (Woodcock, 1990).

Sometimes, as in the 1988 shooting death of aboriginal leader J.J. Harper by a Winnipeg police officer, Chief Akiwenzie's statement is literally true. More generally, his point is that the treatment of aboriginal people by Canada's legal system is deeply unfair: they are still treated as ruffians. The killing of Harper and the miscarriage of justice in the case of Donald

---

4   Ralph Akiwenzie, "We want to do it our way," *The Globe and Mail*, 6 March 1992.

5   See "Georgian Bay" and "Huron" in *The Canadian Encyclopedia*, Volume 2 (Edmonton: Hurtig Publishers, 1985); also, "huron" in *Le Petit Robert* 1, (Paris: SNL – Dictionnaire Le Robert, 1978).

6   A colony was first created on Vancouver Island in 1849; this was expanded to all of British Columbia in 1858. See Woodcock (1990).

Marshall, who spent eleven years in jail for a 1971 murder he did not com-
mit, led to provincial commissions of inquiry. Other (eventually) well-pub-
licized cases of a biased administration of justice included the 1971 sex
murder of Cree teenager Helen Betty Osbourne in Manitoba that went
unpunished for sixteen years and, more recently, the abusive charging, conviction, and imprisonment of Wilson Nepoose in Alberta.

Cases like these, and the many less publicized cases that result in aboriginal men and women being grossly overrepresented in Canada's jails,[7]
prompted Manitoba's 1991 Aboriginal Justice Inquiry to recommend that a
separate aboriginal justice system be developed. Although it has received
considerable support and has become somewhat of a "motherhood" issue,
the prospect of an aboriginal justice system is not a sure thing: not only did
the government of Manitoba reject the recommendation of its Aboriginal
Justice Inquiry, but the then federal Justice Minister also rejected a separate
system, describing it as "a copout," a virtual admission that aboriginals "are
people that cannot be served by the so-called, hypothetical mainstream system." On the other hand, the Saskatchewan government, relying on the
Manitoba inquiry's report, promised to implement a parallel justice system
for aboriginal people.[8] Since then, while many small-scale reforms have been
developing across Canada, no progress has been made on an overall system.

The issue of self-government and that of a separate justice system are
often treated separately. But it should be obvious that the latter is a function
of the former: one of the dimensions of self-government is the collectivity's
ability to sanction deviance. Since the negotiations that led to the
Charlottetown Accord, it is generally recognized by Canada's federal and
provincial governments, and by many Canadians, that aboriginal peoples
have an "inherent right to self-government." This right was, for instance,
re-affirmed by the federal and BC government in the proposed Nisga'a
treaty.[9] But what does this phrase mean, specifically? It is strongly associated

---

7   The Prairie provinces are particularly notorious for their aboriginal representation in jails. In
    Saskatchewan, for instance, while aboriginal people make up 11% of the population, they
    account for 72% of inmates in provincial jails and 34% of inmates in federal prisons; the corre-
    sponding numbers for Manitoba and Alberta are, respectively, 12% / 47% / 40% and 6% / 34%
    / 31%. Quebec is the only province where aboriginal people are underrepresented in jails and
    prisons: 2.2% / 2.0% / 1.7%. Source: "Behind bars," G&M, 19 July 1995, A4; data from
    Correctional Service of Canada, Canadian Centre for Justice Statistics, Federal Department of
    Indian Affairs and Northern Development. On colonialism and aboriginal overrepresentation
    in the justice system, see Monture-Angus (1996).

8   See "Separate native justice rejected for Manitoba," G&M, 29 January 1992; "Separate native
    justice system would be 'copout'," G&M, 31 January 1992;" Saskatchewan moves toward native
    justice," G&M, 1 February 1992.

9   This is, at least, what the governments say: that they recognize the inherent right (see
    Government of Canada, 1995). But their actions, in negotiations with the Nisga'a and others,
    belie that recognition. They insist, for instance, that First Nations self-government be subject
    to the Canadian Charter of Rights and Freedoms. In current conditions, no treaty is possible
    without this framework; such bullying into accepting whitestream practices and authority is
    inconsistent with a serious recognition of the inherent right to self-government.

with the position taken by the Assembly of First Nation, under the leadership of National Chief Ovide Mercredi. In his book *In The Rapids*, Mercredi explains:

> ... our right to govern ourselves does not come from European proclamations or treaties; they just recognized what we were doing already. The Proclamation of 1763 did not create aboriginal land rights – it acknowledged them as pre-existing. We believe, as we are told by our Elders, that our peoples were placed on this land by the Creator, with a responsibility to care for and live in harmony with all her Creation. By living this way, we cared for the Earth, for our brothers and sisters in the animal world and for each other. Fulfilling these responsibilities meant we governed ourselves, and lived a certain way. This is the source of what we call our inherent right of self-government. It has a history that precedes the Charlottetown Accord by more than a millennium. (Mercredi and Turpel, 1993: 31)

Chief Akiwenzie, in his plea in favour of a separate justice system, writes that "... to be equal, native people must be different." That is, an aboriginal administration of justice would function in ways different from whitestream justice. There are already local attempts to accommodate the needs of aboriginal people, going from hiring more native police officers and prison guards, to setting up autonomous band police forces, to altering the functioning of courts and involving elders in sentencing.[10] The experiments, among others, described by Crown attorney Rupert Ross in his book *Dancing with a Ghost* (1992) show that the changes are liable to go far deeper than mere staff replacements. If an aboriginal justice system and self-government do develop, this will have been just a beginning.[11] How deep will the changes be? That the Nisga'a treaty provides a very modest version of a justice system should not hide the fact that other First Nations want much more extensive judicial powers.[12] How extensive might that be? And how would it affect the relationship between whitestream Canadians and aboriginal peoples?

---

10 See for instance "Blood tribe puts own mark on justice system" and "New police grads take posts on reserve," *The Edmonton Journal*, 14 March 1992; a report by Holly Doan on CBC's *Sunday Report*, 19 July 1992; and Ross (1992).

11 In Silverman and Nielsen (1992), see the chapter by Paul Havemann on the limited policy of "indigenization", which might be termed neo-colonial; and on justice in the context of self-government, see the chapter by Marianne O. Nielsen.

12 On the Nisga'a accord, see Introduction, and later in this chapter. Wanting more extensive powers is no guarantee of getting them, however; on a number of scores, the Nisga'a wanted more autonomy than they got. The question remains the willingness of federal and provincial governments to relinquish powers that they have arrogated to themselves.

"We are not like you," Ralph Akiwenzie writes. Leroy Littlebear, lawyer and native studies professor, agrees: "We are different, and don't underestimate the differences we have."[13] And Mary Ellen Turpel (1990) would seem to agree, in writing about "irreconcilable or irreducible elements of human relations." But the point is better made, I think, by Joan Crow; she says, "I'm not you."[14] In this sense, it is not so much difference that matters, as separateness – and indeed wanting to self-govern expresses a will to be separate, autonomous, whether or not you want to do things differently than your neighbour. Chief Akiwenzie might as well have said: We are not you.

In Ovide Mercredi's explanation of the concept of inherent right to self-government, two types of arguments are invoked: one historical, the other cultural. On the one hand, he writes of "what we were doing already" before European occupation of this continent, of "pre-existing" land rights, of inherent right pre-existing the Charlottetown accord "by more than a millennium": the source of the inherent right to self-government is historical precedence. On the other hand, Mercredi outlines what his people did, how they governed themselves: they had the Creator-given responsibility to care for each other and for animal brothers and sisters – "(f)ulfilling these responsibilities meant we governed ourselves, and lived a certain way." Here, he speaks of cultural difference.

In Canadian discussions of aboriginal rights, both these narrative strands are usually present. But the cultural strand often predominates: First Nations should govern themselves, because they are different. The reasons for this predominance are several. Superficially, one might note that cultural difference is more readily visible than a distant historical source. It is underscored, for instance, every time a meeting between whitestream and First Nation representatives begins with what the white stream would describe as an aboriginal religious ceremony. More broadly, the presence of First Nations leaders in the media almost always includes a visual marker of difference, whether in dress, backdrop, or some other element such as the eagle feather that Elijah Harper held in his hand during the final moments of the Meech Lake debate in the Manitoba Legislature. This focus is reinforced in the current context of Canadian politics, which is especially attuned to difference: the First Nations difference is one player of a trio also composed of multiculturalism and gender (with sexual orientation aspiring to turn the trio into a quartet).

There are dangers in emphasizing difference over historical precedence, and it must be remembered that this emphasis is not necessarily deliberately

---

13 In Timothy Appleby, "Separate native justice system would be 'copout'," G&M, 31 January 1992.

14 Joan Crow, "Standing on principle: The constitution and First Nations," *Kinesis*, April 1992: 7, 8.

produced by First Nations representatives. It is at least in part a result of the white stream's receptivity to a rhetoric of difference (see Taylor, 1991). As Robert Young writes, "Western culture has always been defined *against* the limits of others, and culture has always been thought through as a form of cultural difference" (Young, 1995: 93; emphasis added). Modernity, in other words, has relied on a rhetoric of cultural difference to ensure the rule of the white stream over non-European peoples. A rhetoric of gender difference, by the same token, has been a dimension of malestream rule.

In recent years, feminist writers have been particularly sensitive to this danger of difference, because (among other reasons) of the critique of whitestream feminism by women of colour, and the theoretical encounter with poststructuralism. As Barbara Marshall writes, paraphrasing Judith Butler's work, "there is no 'essence' reflected by gender [and race, and culture] – it only takes on a guise of naturalness through repeated, and discursively constructed, performance" (Marshall, 1994: 110). Thus, if recognizing difference is crucial to the furthering of democratic politics, a discourse of difference is at the same time productive of racialized and gendered categories (see for instance Crosby, 1992; Eisenstein, 1994; Marshall, 1994; Mouffe, 1992). The rhetoric of difference is a double-edged sword: a claim to difference can lead to (a degree of) empowerment at the same time that it creates and sustains images of the radical other, who is always subordinate.

The temptation is great to choose sides in this situation. Thus, poststructuralist writers who emphasize the contingency of difference have been criticized for undermining the political struggle of groups (women, African-Americans, people of colour) who stand to gain from the affirmation of their difference (see Fraser, 1989; Marshall, 1994). But the urge to choose sides is very much a case of being caught in a dilemma – and there is nothing good about a dilemma, which is why we say that we may "be caught in" one. The goal ought to be to use "the dilemma to point at the perpendicular," to move from one plane of thought to a more general one (Wu, 1996: 68).[15] In Zen terms, this involves remembering that absolute reality is "nondual reality, which transcends all the pairs of opposites while at the same time embracing them all." (Wu: 68)[16] In poststructuralist terms, it involves remembering that something like "cultural difference" is a discursive construct, which is always sociopolitically situated, and as such performs tasks in the establishment and maintenance (and resistance to) power relations. One ought to adopt a strategic attitude towards it, then, of using it at the same time as undermining its claimed foundations.

---

15 It is both surprising and revealing (of the possibility of intercultural recognition) that Wu is drawing here not only on Zen masters, but also on American Supreme Court Justice Oliver Wendel Holmes.

16 Joseph Couture (1991) similarly emphasizes the non-dualistic character of "native mind."

In this sense, undermining the very notions at the basis of gendered and racialized identities can be seen as a positive contribution to the struggle of subordinated groups. Challenging the naturalness of these identities goes to the generally unchallenged heart of racist and sexist ideologies. And saying that identities are contingent is not saying that they are not real. Their very salience in political discourse is entirely entangled with the fact that inequalities exist, which the dominant needs to justify – women and aboriginal peoples, for instance, have been likened to children, while white males are adults. The whole notion, still current in Canadian law, that "Indians" are wards of the state who need to be "protected" is of a piece with such conceptions (see Frideres, 1988); and the fact is, as Menno Boldt shows, that this supposed protection of "Indian interests" by the federal government has been systematically undercut by appeals to the "national interest" (Boldt, 1993: 68-72). This legal and ideological talk of protection is very much a discourse of difference, at the service of the dominant.

The dominant discourse of difference is also racializing in that it forbids the Other's historicity. The difference must exist from time immemorial, and it is not allowed to change, if it is to be acknowledged as worthy of attention and, indeed, "protection."[17] This is one key reason, for instance, why the Mohawks of Kanesatake have never obtained the establishment of a reserve.[18] The Kanesatake community being outside what has been deemed traditional Mohawk territory, recognition of an aboriginal right to their land has been denied; when the town of Oka appropriated land over the years, the Mohawks were without legal recourse (see York and Pindera, 1991).

The same logic is at work in the *Peters v. Campbell* case. It was important to the Court that syewen be a practice that had existed in basically the same form before the British Crown asserted its sovereignty over "British Columbia." If syewen had developed later, or if it had undergone significant change, its claim to be an aboriginal right would have been seriously undermined. For the purposes of analysis, the Court decided to assume that syewen met that test, and went on to decide that the aboriginal right "at its highest level"[19] was subject to the common law. It did not matter if in fact the pre-existence test was met, because Joseph Peters's initiators had gone

---

17 The Supreme Court of Canada had gone some way toward removing this fixist bias in *R. v. Sparrow* (1990). But in the recent *Van der Peet* (1996) decision, it has reverted to a narrow vision of aboriginal rights as existing only to the extent that the practice in question was "integral" to an aboriginal culture before contact. On these decisions, see Asch (1997).

18 Which would have been a mixed blessing, of course, because of reserves' role in marginalizing and impoverishing First Nations. But in the context of southern Canada's twentieth century, it has been better (or less bad) for an aboriginal community to have a reserve than not.

19 See below for this phrase, its context and an explanation of the Court's reasoning in the *Peters v. Campbell* decision.

beyond what the right might be in the first place. Judge Hood did suggest, however, that he was not convinced that "spirit dancing" as presented to him was the same thing as pre-contact practices – and so, had he chosen to inquire further into the factuality of the right, he might well have found that syewen is not an aboriginal right at all.

On the face of it, this test of pre-existence is absurd and particularly unfair. This is especially visible in regions where contact goes back several hundred years; the more ancient contact is, the less likely it is that "traditional" practices have remained pristine, or even that pre-contact practices can be identified with a high degree of certainty. Besides, there never was such a thing as a pristine traditional practice, for change did occur in aboriginal societies before Europeans showed up.

The situation of the Mohawk people is again instructive. Both Kanewake and Kanesatake were communities established as Catholic missions at the time of New France (Akwesasne was established as an offshoot of Kanewake). Their populations were mixed, with predominantly Mohawk people, but including also Oneida, Huron, "Canadian Algonquian," plus French, English, and Dutch "adoptees" and captives; the practices of these communities, including their spirituality, quickly became an amalgam of Mohawk, European and other cultures (see Demos, 1995).

The first two communities were established on sites chosen by French missionaries without regard for traditional territories. In all three, a new, syncretic culture developed, many features of which (beginning with their specific location) have not existed from time immemorial. Today, all three are considered Mohawk; there are reserves at Kanewake and Akwesasne, but not at Kanesatake. Kanewake and Akwesasne are on the good side of the St.Lawrence River – on the side, that is, identified as traditional Mohawk territory, which legally entitled the communities to an aboriginal right to the land. Eventually, reserves were created on portions of that territory. Thanks to the location of the missionaries' grant from François 1, Kanesatake, as already noted, was outside Mohawk territory, on the wrong side of the St.Lawrence,[20] and according to the pre-existence test could claim no aboriginal right. It just so happened, then, that Kanesatake was particularly unlucky, and is still paying for it today. The "Oka crisis" and its aftermath, of course, are a direct outcome of this situation.

More recent contact between aboriginal peoples and Europeans has also produced alterations to "traditional" practices. Syewen as it is practised today on Vancouver Island and elsewhere, in the context of the Winter Dance, would appear to be one such amalgam. According to anthropologists (Amoss, 1978; Suttles, 1987), it integrates certain elements that previ-

---

20 Kanesatake and Oka are on the north shore of the Lac-Des-Deux-Montagnes, which is to the immediate north-west of the island of Montreal, at the confluence of the St-Lawrence and Ottawa rivers.

ously were specific to the potlatch: having both been forbidden by federal law, key elements of the Winter Dance and of the potlatch were merged so as to make their practice possible despite the ban. As well, the introduction of Christianity, and especially of the Shaker sect, among First Nations of the Pacific Coast at the end of the nineteenth century seems to have influenced the form of the rituals practised at the Winter Dance. And finally, the social control function of syewen in cases involving "social illnesses" (as lawyer Lara Skye would have it) is particularly salient in the context of oppression which has produced so much alcoholism, substance abuse, and violence against women, to mention but a few. Thus, while no one doubts that syewen is a genuinely and specifically aboriginal practice and considering that it has developed to what it is today as a form of adaptation / resistance to whitestream domination, is it not particularly appalling that it might have been denied the status of aboriginal right, had it not been ruled subject to the common law in the first place?

Oppression is compounded by the pre-existence test, through which the white stream insists on the cultural stagnation of First Nations. In Kanesatake, the message is: if you do not change, we will give you a reserve, but if you do, you cannot count on even that. The practitioners of syewen were presented with the same kind of double jeopardy: we are going to truncate your presumed right to make it fit within the common law, but since you have been changing / adapting / resisting, we might decide later to take away what we are hypothetically granting now.

As absurd and egregiously unfair as it is, the pre-existence test is constitutive of whitestream conceptions of self, which require that only European peoples truly have a history; others must be static. This is one way in which the origin of the anthropological concept of "culture" is racist, at the same time as it has played a role in the structuring of academic disciplines: Western peoples have "history," which is studied in History Departments, while other peoples have "culture," which is studied in Anthropology Departments.[21] It is important, in this sense, that groups struggling for equality not rely exclusively and uncritically on their culture and difference, but also that they claim their history, for it is their historicity that is most destabilizing of whitestream domination.

If we remove the whitestream monopoly on historicity, there remains no reason why an aboriginal right should be recognized only if it can be proven that a practice exists as part of an unbroken continuum (or even unchanged) since before contact. Cultural difference, then, is relativised as we recognize it as an historical process rather than a static, natural, racial constant. And a more realistic analysis of contact can be made: clearly, the cultures of abo-

---

21 In this scheme, China and India are problematic only to some degree, for they (it has been claimed) have been static for centuries. On the racist origins of the concept "culture" and of the structuring of academic disciplines, see Young (1995).

riginal peoples have been transformed by contact, and so have whitestream cultures (although fewer people would be aware of that; see Weatherford, 1991). For good and bad, there is something of the white stream in aboriginal cultures today, and vice versa, because peoples change through history.

It has been difficult to say this out loud in the current Canadian context, because so much of the First Nations' political capital rests on their affirmation of difference, including the pressure of the legal test of pre-existence. But this test itself is oppressive of First Nations today, and it must be discredited. This done, it would not be politically important that First Nations are different: their autonomy, their inherent right to self-government can and should be established on the basis of their history, of the historical fact of their sovereignty.[22] In that sovereign context, First Nations could choose to be as different as they want, without the whitestream pressure to ahistorical difference as a means to (subordinated) autonomy.

● ● ●

Frank Campbell and several others were sued for "assault, battery, and false imprisonment." Since they agreed that the events claimed by Peters had indeed taken place, their defence was to direct the Court's attention elsewhere: to the grounds upon which they were being dragged in front of a Canadian court of law. This is how the issue was presented by the defendant's counsel to Judge Hood, who duly noted the question in his decision: "Are the individual rights of aboriginal persons subject to the collective rights of the aboriginal nation to which he belongs?" (160) This goes to the heart of the right to self-government. If the answer is yes, claimed the defence, then the Supreme Court of British Columbia has no jurisdiction in the conflict between Joseph Peters and his initiators. The defense answered yes to its own question, of course, in favour of aboriginal collective rights. To do so, it appealed to section 35(1) of the *Constitution Act, 1982*, which states: "The existing aboriginal and treaty rights of the aboriginal peoples of Canada are hereby recognized and affirmed."

This defense was, in essence, a challenge to the rules of the game that allowed a law suit to proceed between these parties, and that gave Canadian courts the authority to adjudicate upon it. But Judge Hood missed this basic point, not seeing that his very jurisdiction was at issue. He did rule on the defence's contention that the individual rights of an aboriginal person are subject to aboriginal collective rights. He disagreed:

---

22 Let's not confuse the two historical arguments. The source of the inherent right to self-government is that aboriginal peoples were on this continent a very long time ago, sovereign and doing a variety of things. The pre-existence test (for the recognition of an aboriginal right) requires that aboriginal peoples show that they are doing now the exact same things that they were doing centuries ago.

> Assuming that spirit dancing was an aboriginal right, and that it existed and was practised prior to the assertion of British sovereignty over Vancouver Island, and the imposition of English law, in my opinion those aspects of it which were contrary to English common law, such as the use of force, assault, battery and wrongful imprisonment, did not survive the coming into force of that law.... (160)

"Spirit dancing," in other words, could perhaps be an aboriginal right, but only to the extent that its components do not contravene English law. There is no ambiguity in the Court's decision to affirm "the supremacy of English law to the exclusion of all others," and thus the "paramountcy of common law to the alleged aboriginal right" (160).[23] Judge Hood found for the plaintiff, Joseph Peters. In doing so, the Court exercised cultural authority at its most self-assured — where cultural authority is defined by aboriginal legal scholar Mary Ellen Turpel, as:

> ... the authority which one culture is seen to possess to create law and legal language to resolve disputes involving other cultures and the manner in which it explains (or fails to explain) and sustains its authority over different peoples. (Turpel, 1990: 4)

The Globe and Mail paraphrased the ruling in these terms, which are partly a quote from Judge Hood, himself quoting the defense's key question: "The freedoms and civil rights of an aboriginal Canadian are not subject to the collective rights of the aboriginal nation to which he belongs" (GM 1). By referring to the plaintiff as an "aboriginal Canadian," the reporter caught very well the logic of the ruling. In the introduction to his decision, Judge Hood had identified the plaintiff, Joseph Peters, as "an 'Indian' within the meaning of the *Indian Act*, R.S.C. (1985), c. 1-5, and (...) of course, a Canadian citizen" (140). This "of course" had been a good indication that the Court would consider the plaintiff as a Canadian first and foremost. Aboriginal rights, whatever they may be or amount to, must function within that framework:

---

23 The reasoning underpinning the decision is less clear. Relying mainly on three historic decisions (*Delgamuukw v. The Queen* (1989), 38 BCLR (2D); *Regina v. Sparrow* [1990] 70 DLR (4th); *Saumur v. City of Quebec* [1953] 2 SCR), Judge Hood noted that "just as rights guaranteed under the Charter are *not absolute*, those guaranteed under s. 35 are not absolute"; he then affirmed, contradictarily it seems to me, that the plaintiff "lives in a free society and his rights *are inviolable*" (161, 162; emphasis added). My purpose here is not, however, to evaluate the internal consistency of the court's legal reasoning; it is, rather, to situate it in its inter-cultural context.

Placing the aboriginal right at *its highest level* it does not include civil immunity for coercion, force, assault, unlawful confinement, or any other unlawful tortious conduct on the part of the defendants, in forcing the plaintiff to participate in their tradition. While the plaintiff may have special rights and status in Canada as an Indian, the "original" rights and freedoms he enjoys can be no less than those enjoyed by fellow citizens, Indian and non-Indian alike. He lives in a free society and his rights are inviolable. (...) His freedoms and rights are not "subject to the collective rights of the aboriginal nation to which he belongs." (162; emphasis added)

Judge Hood thought, then, that Joseph Peters would have had "less" rights than other Canadians if it had been the case that his were subordinated to the collective rights of the Coast Salish nation. Being subject to the collective rights of the Canadian state, on the other hand, would be a guarantee that Peters's individual rights are "no less than those enjoyed by fellow citizens." Coming from a judge working in a federal context, this reasoning would be surprising if the discourse of rights in Canada were not as ideological as it is. Since the Charter of Rights and Freedoms came into effect in 1985, there has developed a widespread belief among (English-speaking) Canadians that if individual rights are not protected in a pan-Canadian way by the Charter, they are not protected at all. In this sense as in others, the Charter is in conflict with Canada's federalism, in that it undermines the autonomy of the federated units.

In order to be specific, let me make a little detour toward Quebec and its Bill 101. Adopted in 1977, well before the Canadian Charter of Rights was written, and applying to a variety of the Quebec government's jurisdictions, it respected the rules of Canada's constitutional game that were then in place.[24] It did place restrictions on individual rights, on the grounds that it was reasonable to do so because of the vulnerability of Quebec's French culture. At about the same time, the Quebec government adopted its own *Charte des droits et libertés de la personne* – again, before the Canadian Charter – that could be used to challenge provincial laws and regulations. Other provinces and the federal government also adopted, at various times, laws protecting individual rights; each federated unit developed rights protections applying to its respective jurisdictions. Provincial jurisdiction, then, does not result in Canadians from various provinces having "less" rights than they would have otherwise. Rather, provincial jurisdiction means that individual rights are formulated and regulated at the level of the province. The

---

24 With the notable exception of Article 133 of the BNA *Act* of 1867, which made French and English the official languages of Quebec's legislature, laws, regulations, and courts. The dispositions of Bill 101 contravening this obligation were declared unconstitutional in 1979 by the Supreme Court of Canada in PG *Quebec v. Blaikie*. See Woehrling (1993).

Canadian Charter comes as an addition to this situation, overlapping in many cases with provincial codes, and taking precedence in all cases because it is constitutionalized.

The claim for "the collective rights of the aboriginal nation" is of a similar type: jurisdiction over the individual rights of members of the Coast Salish nation should belong to the Coast Salish community. Only the belief that the Coast Salish nation has no respect for individual autonomy can lead one to think that recognizing its collective right would result in "less" individual rights for its members.[25]

One of the challenges to Bill 101 that became (in)famous involved commercial signs: the law mandated that French be the only language on signs. Store owners brought a suit to the Quebec Superior Court claiming that freedom of expression and the right to equality were being violated. The Court agreed that freedom of expression was breached, citing for the most part violations of Quebec's *Charte des droits et libertés* (as well as of the Canadian Charter of Rights). This judgement was later confirmed by the Supreme Court of Canada (see Woehrling, 1993). So on the basis of the Quebec *Charte*, a Quebec court ruled that a Quebec law violated individual rights and therefore had to be modified. The Canadian Charter was also invoked, but this was superfluous, for the Quebec *Charte* was doing the job anyway.[26] The same kind of process can – and indeed does – occur for the laws and regulations of other provinces and of the federal government. Rights, then, are protected in a federated manner.

What is the purpose of the Canadian Charter in this context? It inserts rights protection into the Constitution, resulting in its application to all jurisdictions (federal and provincial). In Canada's federal structure, this is highly unusual: federal laws are binding on the federal government only, a province's laws are binding on that province only, but the Charter is binding on all governments. This pan-Canadian reach fosters a One-Canada patriotism and identity that undermine the autonomy of the (provincial) federated units, by feeding the belief that the only rights that matter (and are protected) are pan-Canadian Charter rights.

This fostering of Canadian patriotism was an overt goal of the makers of the Charter, and in this it can be said that they have succeeded beautifully. But this enhanced patriotism meshes nicely with the resistance against recognizing Quebec's distinctiveness and with the racism that underlies the

---

25 Unless aboriginal protection of rights were constitutionalized, such protection would however be less legally secure than that afforded by the constitutionalized Canadian Charter. Which is not to say that it would be less culturally secure.

26 Legal scholar Michael Mandel writes that in order to do this job, the wording of the Quebec *Charte* had to be twisted out of recognition, for political reasons (see Mandel, 1994: 162). Whether or not this is the case, the fact is that the *Charte* was made to do this job – what it took was the political will on the part of the Court.

decades-long attempt at assimilating "Indians." Thus, if the Charter, on one side, makes Canadians feel good about themselves and their civilization, it serves, on the flip side, to delegitimize the aspirations of Quebecers and First Nations. It is in this context that one may understand the angry reaction of many British Columbians who are condemning the Nisga'a agreement, because it denies the precept of "one law for all."

Contrary to what most Canadians like to believe, then, Canada has not been uniformly moving away from colonialism in the past decade or so. One of the ideological effects of the Charter is to foster a commitment to sameness that undercuts their ability to make sense of what Quebecers and First Nations want.[27] The Charter encourages Canadians to think in ways that result in intolerance toward the autonomy that both these national groups have been seeking within Canada. In this sense, the hardening of opinion since the late 1980s against Quebec's search for autonomy is not merely accidental; it is a systemic effect of Charter ideology. The same goes for attitudes towards aboriginal self-government.

Judges are people too. As everyone else, they are subject to ideological constructions that are pushing federalism into the Charter's background. This is striking in a case such as *Peters v. Campbell*, because the Charter did not come into play: Peters was claiming common law rights. The defendants, for their part, were claiming aboriginal rights set out in Canada's *Constitution Act, 1982*. No matter, Judge Hood reverted to Charter logic in his claim that the only way for Joseph Peters's rights to be protected was by treating him as any other Canadian, over the heads of legislatures, parliament, and, of course, "the aboriginal nation to which he belongs."

•   •   •

The central conflict narrated in the Court's decision on *Peters v. Campbell* was indeed that between "aboriginal rights" and "individual civil rights." The presence of this polarity in *Peters v. Campbell* was made possible by the existence in Canadian law of dispositions relating to both these rights. On the one hand, the Charter and a whole body of common law address individual rights; on the other hand, Canadian law also has much to say about aboriginals in Sections 25, 35 and 37(2) of the *Constitution Act, 1982*, in treaties and court decisions, and in the *Indian Act*. But had there been no mention of aboriginal rights in at least one area of Canadian law, no defence in front of a Canadian court challenging the rules of the game would have been thinkable. The defence would have been reduced to arguing about the questions: Was there assault, battery, and false imprisonment? Was there consent?

---

27 This is so despite clauses in the Charter that recognize the collective rights of linguistic minorities, and Part II of the *Constitution Act, 1982*, which recognizes aboriginal collective rights.

The first line of defense for the initiators of Joseph Peters was stated thus by Judge Hood: "The defendants deny that they assaulted, battered or falsely imprisoned the plaintiff." Three more lines of defense follow: "first, lack of intention on their part to inflict harm on the plaintiff, second, consent or acquiescence on the part of the plaintiff, and third, a constitutional defense" based on their aboriginal rights (141).

While consistent with the standard practice in litigation of defendants making both general and specific denials of the facts alleged, the first defense could seem incomprehensible given what we know about the uncontested facts of the initiation. The same goes for the second defense, about the lack of intent. And both certainly were quickly dispatched by Judge Hood: "I do not propose to deal at length with (...) the tort issues. (...) The plaintiff has proven, beyond any question, almost continuous assault, battery, and wrongful or false imprisonment during his ordeal" (150). But it is crucial to realize that these defenses do not merely assert statements of facts (no assault occurred, etc.). Rather, they assert an aboriginal perspective on the facts; to put it in a nutshell, the dancers did not intend to assault, batter and imprison, they intended to initiate and help. From their point of view, which is not idiosyncratic or merely self-exculpatory but rather culturally constructed, they did not assault. They initiated.

The point here is that "assault" and "initiation" are not natural facts, which are directly grasped as such by dancers, judges and newspaper readers; they are, rather, particular descriptions of the world, expressing particular cultures. In claiming that no assault occurred and that there was no intent to assault, the defense was saying that even the most basic tools (such as acts defined in law as "assault," "battery," etc.) of the Canadian legal system are inadequate for dealing with the events surrounding the initiation of Joseph Peters.

The defense was inviting the court to declare itself incompetent. But Judge Hood did not quite grasp this. He did not, that is, understand that in a situation such as the Peters initiation, the aboriginal right claimed makes "assault, battery, and false imprisonment" irrelevant descriptions of the world and therefore renders Canadian courts incompetent. This incomprehension is well indicated by his puzzlement at why the defendants chose to appeal to s.35(1) of the Constitution, on aboriginal right, rather than to s.25 and common law rights, on freedom of religion (157). But in the end, Judge Hood could afford to not understand, because his description of the world rules over the Coast Salish people's description of the world.

If a law suit was to be fought, then, over Joseph Peters's misadventure, there existed a whole set of textual-legal resources for it to be fought over the issue of Indian vs White, aboriginal right vs civil right, on terms defined and dictated by the whitestream side of the relationship. Within the current Canadian legal framework, it was easy to bring a suit of civil wrong, it was possible to mount a constitutional defense based on s.35, and it was easy for the court to proclaim the supremacy of English law – to assert the cultural authority of the occident over aboriginal peoples. More specifically, it was easy and natural for the court to consider (at least certain aspects of) syewen as a tort, and even as a crime although this was a civil proceeding. Judge Hood is worth quoting at length here:

> I am not satisfied that even an ancient tradition or activity carried on by the defendants and their ancestors, which involves force, assault, injury and confinement, all against the will of the initiate, can be said to be a continuing aboriginal right. If spirit dancing includes *criminal* conduct as an integral part of it, it could not be said to be an aboriginal right which survived the introduction of English law into the colonies. In this regard I note that under the Criminal Code both assault and confinement of a person are criminal offenses in certain circumstances. (…) In my opinion, conduct amounting to civil wrongs (rights from the point of view of the person wronged) should stand on the same footing as criminal conduct. If such conduct cannot be separated from the spirit dancing, and thus is an integral part of it, then in my opinion spirit dancing is not an aboriginal right recognized or protected by the law. (156; emphasis added)

Because of his automatic assertion of cultural authority, it was of no importance to Judge Hood that, within the Coast Salish description of the world, it is indeed quite possible that nothing other than a proper initiation occurred, and that it was done for perfectly good reasons. This fact, that the propriety of the initiation is (necessarily) ruled irrelevant by a Canadian court, results in exposing its constitutive inability to do justice to aboriginal life.[28]

The main conflict in *Peters v. Campbell* (but not the only one: see Chapter 5) stems from the assertion by the Canadian state of cultural authority over aboriginal ways. Put differently: faced with alleged "deviant" behaviour by an individual, the Canadian state claims a monopoly on the authority to sanction it. Again: what the Canadian state could not tolerate in the initiation of Joseph Peters was less the initiation itself, than its being carried out independently of its own authority. If the fundamental task of self-government is to ensure that First Nations are able to conduct their lives in the context of their own cultures and make their own decisions about what is good for them, then a key test of any self-government system is whether or

---

28 I am concerned here with the self-government question "what community has jurisdiction over whose individual rights?"; this issue is distinct from whether or not, according to Coast Salish culture, the initiators were justified in disregarding Joseph Peters's lack of consent. On that question, see Chapters 3, 5 and 6.

not it would leave the conflict between Joseph Peters and his initiators to be decided among First Nations people, through an aboriginal process.

Assuming that an agreement such as that of the Nisga'a (which is widely seen as establishing the model for self-government in BC) had been in place between the Coast Salish Nation, Canada, and BC, what would have happened to the *Peters v. Campbell* case? Could Peters have pulled out by claiming non-membership? Could his lack of consent to being initiated have been legitimately overruled by the Coast Salish community? In the Nisga'a agreement, when non-members of the Nisga'a Nation have dealings with the judiciary, they are given the option of either going to the Nisga'a or the BC court systems; and a non-citizen who has agreed to the Nisga'a Court's authority has to further agree if the penalty is other than "those generally imposed by provincial or superior courts in Canada" (Government of Canada et al., 15 February 1996: 88). Finally, when anyone's potential sentence is prison, that person may also choose the BC court.[29]

If the Nisga'a agreement does turn out to be an influential model for future self-government agreements, the claims of the aboriginal justice system will be highly dependent on whether the person brought to justice is a First Nation citizen. In the Nisga'a agreement, a person is entitled to citizenship through either ancestry or adoption, and may therefore enroll as an official member of the Nation; this person has to apply for enrollment and, once a member, may resign his or her membership.[30] In that context, a person who seriously does not want to be a member of the First Nation would have either not applied for enrollment or would have resigned her membership. But someone who is on the First Nation's official enrolment register could not claim in court that s/he does not belong to the aboriginal community. On the other hand, someone may have clear links to the community, as Peters did (being the son of a prominent Coast Salish family, and being the spouse of a Coast Salish woman who asked the community that he be initiated), but have chosen to stay off the register. In the Nisga'a accord, such a person would not be considered a member of the Nisga'a nation, at least for the purpose of adjudicating conflicts.

Given all this, what kind of help to the Salish community would Nisga'a-type self-government have been in the case of *Peters v. Campbell*? First, in

---

29 See Government of Canada, Province of British Columbia and Nisga'a Tribal Council, *Nisga'a Treaty Negotiations: Agreement-in-Principle*, 15 February, 1996. In the Chapter on "Administration of Justice," paragraphs 32C and 33 limit the Nisga'a Court's jurisdiction to Nisga'a citizens except when the person accepts its authority; and paragraph 36 limits the type of penalties the Nisga'a Court may impose on non-citizens to whitestream practices. Further, paragraph 35 offers any accused person the option of going to the Provincial Court of British Columbia if the penalty may be emprisonment.

30 See *Nisga'a Treaty Negotiations: Agreement-in-Principle*, "Eligibility and Enrolment," paragraphs 2, 5, and 10.

order to be treated as an ordinary Canadian citizen, Peters would have had to stay off the register in advance of his conflict with his initiators. Had he done so, any action by his initiators would have been subject to his consent. Had they initiated him without his consent, he could have sued them in front of the BC Supreme Court and won – just as he actually did. On the other hand, had he previously applied for and obtained citizenship in the Coast Salish nation, things get complicated. We have first to remember that an initiation is not a punishment. So, the Coast Salish justice system might have become involved only after the initiation, to deal with Peters's complaint against his initiators. But remember that in the Nisga'a accord, self-government remains subject to the Canadian Charter of Rights and Freedoms. So, Peters could just as well have gone to the BC Supreme Court and claimed that his rights under the common law and the Charter had been violated – and he likely would have won.

Under the Nisga'a regime, then, the integrity of such traditional practices as syewen remains vulnerable to the consent at any time of the person who is being "helped," and who may well be considered deviant by the community. In other words, under the Nisga'a regime, the outcome of the Peters initiation could easily have been the same as what actually happened: a whitestream lawsuit would have delegitimated syewen as a means of social control, and therefore destructured the Salish people as a self-governing community.

● ● ●

It should be clear, at this point, that we should not assume that a system of aboriginal justice would merely mirror the current whitestream system, but with a staff of aboriginal men and women, that judges, cops, prison guards, etc. would do basically the same jobs but would be "Indians." We have seen that initiations without consent should be seen as dealing with individuals in need of spiritual healing rather than as dealing with criminals. No judges, cops or prisons are needed for this, which is not to say that they would completely disappear.

Modernity and aboriginality have different institutional ways of exercising social control over deviance. Because of this, if an aboriginal justice system is to genuinely function according to aboriginal criteria, it seems necessary for it to be established in the context of wide-ranging aboriginal self-government – and it is far from clear that the Nisga'a accord goes far enough in that direction. Social control within First Nations is likely to distribute normality and deviance in ways different from those of modernity: some people may be labelled deviant in one context but not in the other, and some deviants whom modernity would allocate to its justice system would, for example, be subjected to aboriginal spiritual and/or therapeutic processes.

There would undoutedly be fewer aboriginal men and women in jail, among other reasons[31] because fewer would be treated as criminals and more as wounded spirits. The revitalisation of aboriginal spiritual traditions, in the last several years, is a sign that many aboriginal communities would be equipped to meet the challenge. Chances are that this will result in more harmony in aboriginal communities, and between aboriginal people and whitestream Canadians. But there are prerequisites for this to work as well as it can, for this to happen at all: that whitestream Canadians have more understanding of, trust in, and respect for, aboriginal ways and that we not jump to conclusions of barbarity at the first occasion.

In the case of *Peters v. Campbell*, at least a minimal understanding of Coast Salish cultural practices (including such things as collective decision-making and healing rituals) is the only way to realize that, at least potentially, the initiation was neither arbitrary, an "assault, battery, and false imprisonment," nor an imposition by a community on someone who is not part of it. One may realize, then, that an aboriginal self-government endowed with sufficient authority to rule over such a situation would be quite well-equipped to deal with it.

Responding to a statement by the defendants' counsel to the effect that "the application of the common law approach to their activity has had a profound negative affect [sic] on the whole of the Coast Salish Nation," Judge Hood found it "questionable whether in fact the common law does necessarily infringe on the Aboriginal right" (157). In other words, while syewen itself may be a right, conducting a forced initiation may not be an integral part of that right, without even having to consider issues of common law. This is clearly absurd, as it ignores the role that syewen obviously plays (at least in some cases) as a form of social control. The only option left, then, is to limit the practice of syewen to its consenting (and most frequent) variant by claiming the paramountcy of the common law, which is exactly what Judge Hood ends up doing. This substantiates the defence's claim that the common law approach is injurious to the whole Coast Salish Nation, as should be obvious anyway, since its own cultural practices are superseded by foreign ones.

Judge Hood could have found how culturally important the integrity of syewen is by paying serious attention to Amoss's *Coast Salish Spirit Dancing*, which the defence provided him. And he needed not search any further than *The Canadian Encyclopedia* to find that syewen is at the core of a religious revival among Northwest Coast peoples; that its practice is accounted for in "institutional myths," which are one of the three main types of myths

---

31 On the Louis Bull reserve in central Alberta, since a fully autonomous aboriginal police force was created seven years ago, the crime rate is reported to have dropped by 60%. Asked to account for this improvement, a local cop suggested that there was now more respect for the law among band members. CBC's *Sunday Report*, 19 July 1992.

of aboriginal peoples in Canada; and that it is one instance of the Guardian Spirit Quest, which "once occurred throughout most of the tribal groups in Canada."[32] The fact that this Quest is largely a thing of the past is the result of exactly the type of cultural authority which Judge Hood exercised so serenely. Not seeing that to subject syewen to the common law is destructive of Coast Salish culture, is to display just the kind of arrogant ignorance that has come so close to destroying aboriginal peoples.

---

32 Articles on "Native People, Northwest Coast" and "Native People, Religion," *The Canadian Encyclopedia*.

Chapter 5
Gender equality

My rights stop at the point where they infringe upon your rights: this notion, classically formulated in J.S. Mill's *On Liberty*, is perhaps the best known statement of the liberal discourse on individual rights. It also informs legal decisions by courts with regard to conflicts between individuals, such as contract and family disputes.

Yet strangely – or perhaps not so strangely – this inter-individual concern quickly disappears from view when complaints like that of Joseph Peters are made. In such cases, as we have seen, the rights of an individual tend to be pitted against "collective rights." But just as this latter opposition often serves rhetorical purposes that are not well suited to understanding the conflict at hand, forgetting the relationships between individuals is a sure way to miss the point of many rights claims.

As constructed in Court (and repeated in the media), the legal action by Joseph Peters involved three main players: Peters himself, claiming rights as a Canadian citizen; his initiators, claiming collective aboriginal rights under the Canadian constitution; and the Canadian state, represented by the Court and claiming a monopoly on legitimate violence. But the argument by Joseph Peters that his individual rights were violated by the Coast Salish community is not the whole story. When members of the Longhouse grabbed and initiated him against his will, they were intervening in a conflict between Peters and his wife, Pat Michaels. She is the fourth, indispensable player in the story.

Alongside the self-government question of whether the Longhouse members were entitled to initiate him, then, there is the issue of the relationship between Peters and Michaels, a relationship which she, at least, thought suffered from severe problems. Indeed, when Peters undertook legal action, he sued not only Frank Campbell and six other initiators and elders, but also two bands and Pat Michaels. These latter suits were eventually dropped, but their initial filing is indicative of Peters's (and/or his lawyer's) understanding of the conflict in which he found himself.

Taking individual rights seriously in this case thus requires careful consideration of how Pat Michaels's rights come into play. This was not done by the Court, *The Globe and Mail*, or *Western Report*. As for the Islandtown newspapers, they were more than oblique in their references to Pat Michaels. In one article (RN 2), *The Regional News* referred to the initiation being intended as "atonement" for Peters leaving his wife and children, and quoted the RCMP staff sergeant's suggestive comment on Peters's character: "(he) knows the ins and outs of the law ... Either he should launch an investigation or keep his mouth shut."

● ● ●

The Peters / Michaels relationship is not simply one between individuals; it is mediated by gender. I have already argued that the fact that Joseph Peters is a man made a strong contribution to his forced initiation becoming a judicial and media event. Further, the description in the media of Peters being stripped naked out-of-doors introduces an element of sexual humiliation which makes his initiation all the more spectacular and objectionable to whitestream readers. Not that there is something inherently "sexual" about being naked, but nakedness in whitestream North America is strongly sexually marked. Unexpectedly perhaps, such a sexualization is often an important element in the construction of national imagined communities: "Newspapers, film, novels and theater all create sexed bodies as public spectacles, thereby helping to instill through representational practices an erotic investment in the national romance" (Parker et al., 1992: 12).

The near invisibility of Pat Michaels in Judge Hood's decision and in media accounts of the conflict also stems from a gendered logic: the fact that she is a woman makes her rights count for less, and allows the spotlight to be squarely on her husband. This is not unusual. Research on gender and the media has shown that it is generally a struggle for women to be seen and heard on the public stage (see Stone, 1993), other, one might add, than as "sexed bodies."

The gender nexus in the story is indeed the key that allows us to unlock the riddle of the initiators' motivations, which are the basis of their decision to override Joseph Peters's individual rights, in the context of their aboriginal right to govern themselves. For this unlocking to happen, however, it is necessary to respect Pat Michaels as an autonomous agent just as much as we clearly are prepared to respect Joseph Peters's autonomy. In the Court's decision and the media, however, she gets no such respect.

For reasons that are not made clear in the judgement, Michaels seemed reluctant to testify; she repeatedly claimed that she could not remember various events and conversations in which she had taken part. The elders who had been in charge of the initiation had also been reluctant to testify, especially on the specifics of what the initiation involved. This reluctance of the elders had elicited a degree of sympathy on the part of Judge Hood, whose account of testimony did not dwell on their silences. It is safe to assume that the sources of Pat Michaels's reluctance were similar to those of the elders: she did not want the Supreme Court of British Columbia to be dealing with family and Coast Salish matters. When she had needed help, she chose to go to the Coast Salish community, and not to whitestream institutions, which were now being used by her estranged husband against her and those who helped her.[1] But whereas Judge Hood rather deferred to the elders' quietness, he showed no such sympathy toward Michaels. He narrated at length and with evident impatience her claims to a failing memory. Her credibility thus undermined, she slid to the margin of the story.

It is in fact quite remarkable that women are both central and peripheral in the story of the initiation of Joseph Peters. That is, two women played absolutely key roles in the events but, at various junctures, they are either written out of the story or their part in it is denigrated. The two women are Pat Michaels, of course, and Joanne Pelkey, Joseph Peters's aunt.[2] But contrary to the Indian vs White narrative, which was in the foreground of the Court decision and of media reports, this gender dimension (in which women are marginalized and humiliated) is only written in the background of the story as told by Judge Hood and the media. Without the benefit of close reading, it is very much in danger of going unseen. And as the gender nexus remains unseen, so do the elders' reasons for conducting the initiation, a double invisibility that enacts, as we will see, the intertwining of gender and colonial oppression.

● ● ●

We should never forget or understimate the fact that, after all, it is Pat Michaels who set the events in motion. She thought that she and her husband needed help, and so she went to the elders of the Longhouse to ask that he be initiated. The elders responded to her request by requiring the authorization of a family member. Roger Andrews, an elder and a defendant, testified that "'before we could do anything she would have to get permission from someone in the family.' He suggested that she obtain permission either from the plaintiff's brother Gary, or from his aunt, Mrs. Joanne Pelkar

---

1   On the difficulty for a non-aboriginal person to read the aboriginal context, in particular when gender relations are concerned, see R.A. Williams (1992).

2   In the judgement, Judge Hood refers to her as Joanne Pelkar. But I found out while researching the case that "Pelkar" is a misspelling and that the correct spelling is Pelkey. (Remember that I am working with aliases: I am transposing Judge Hood's mistake.)

[sic]" (145).

Another elder and defendant, Moe Johnson, also testified that they required Pat Michaels to "have the consent of the plaintiff's family," and that she may go to either his brother or his aunt (147). This is odd and interesting: wasn't Pat Michaels herself a close family member? Why should someone else's permission be needed? It seems that, because they did not know her at the time (according to the testimony of Roger Andrews), the elders dismissed the possibility that she may grant authorization; a family member known to them, then, had to authorize the initiation.

So, Pat Michaels sought Joanne Pelkey's authorization. Ms. Pelkey, herself a member of the Longhouse, made her authorization conditional on that of Joseph Peters's brother Gary. In doing this, she removed herself from the events by making her authorization redundant. Pat Michaels did not, apparently, obtain Gary Peters's authorization. But she went back to the elders claiming that she did and they evidently believed her. There is no account in the judgement of why Michaels did not go to her brother-in-law; it could be that their relationship was not such that he would likely help her. In any case, the elders, after evaluating the situation and armed (they thought) with proper authorization, went ahead with the initiation. In her testimony as narrated by Judge Hood, Pat Michaels did not challenge this sequence of events.

The gender dynamic in this colonial story is striking. To begin with, the coerced initiation of Joseph Peters was a response to Pat Michaels's appeal for help. After this starting point, however, women disappear from the story. First, being (apparently) unknown to the elders, Michaels was not considered a proper family member for the purpose of authorizing the initiation; and Joanne Pelkey, a proper authority, wanted nothing to do with her nephew's problems. She would testify in Court that she did not associate much with the family.[3] Second, when the initiation was brought to the BC Supreme Court, where the initiators' motivations are considered irrelevant, the story was all about the violation of Peters's rights and Michaels was the only witness to be portrayed in an unfavourable light. Third, when the Court's take on the conflict was reported in the media, the erasure of women was repeated, producing a narrative where native culture displays a gross disrespect for the rights of this man, Joseph Peters. This male-centred, racist narrative is very much an expression of dominant Eurocentric practice: on the one hand, it is taken for granted that men are autonomous selves, with control over the integrity of their body; on the other hand, the extent to which women are autonomous selves remains an issue, and especially so when it comes to control over the integrity of their body.

---

3 On this issue, more below.

Within the Coast Salish community, a group of men acted on behalf of Pat Michaels (and, despite himself, of Joseph Peters). Once the conflict is captured by colonialist discourse, in Court and the media, however, women and their concerns are pushed into demeaning irrelevance, leaving visible only the suspension of a man's rights. One may be sceptical of the notion that the initiators were operating on Pat Michaels's behalf: not only were they attempting to heal Joseph Peters, but the elders did not consider Michaels a sufficient authority to override his consent. How is this consistent with a claim that this woman's rights counted for much in her Coast Salish community?

In the Report of the Royal Commission on Aboriginal Peoples, one reads that when a community member was experiencing problems, "(s)etting the problem right was a concern of the whole community, and ceremonialists, medicine persons or shamans were the agents called upon to diagnose the problem and restore balance *on behalf of the community*" (Canada, 1996A: 629; emphasis added). This should be read as: on behalf of all people involved, one of whom in this case is Pat Michaels, and another is Joseph Peters. In other words, we don't have to interpret the situation as pitting the interests of one individual against those of another: both are served.

Still, one may argue: yes, but it remains important to know who the elders and initiators meant to help. This is what would enable us to determine to what extent the needs of women can be met in aboriginal communities. With all due caveats as to the interpretation and importance of overt intentions, let us suppose that the elders sought to "restore balance on behalf of the community." In what ways is this answer unsatisfactory to one who wants to ensure that the needs of women are met? The issue, I would argue, turns on whether "the community" is conceptualized (by its members) as including women as full members. In communities where this is the case, women are likely to be well served by actions undertaken "on behalf of the community," and they are likely to be ill served in cases where their place is not fully honoured.

What of this case, though? Were the elders and initiators seeking to help her, or were they solely (or even primarily) concerned with the welfare of Joseph Peters? Given the documentation on which this book is built, this question is to some extent unanswerable. However, it can be said that:

1. the initiators wanted to heal him, and as such were acting on *his* behalf;

2. by healing her husband, they were simultaneously helping *her*;

3. all of this as a result of *her* call for help. That the elders sought further guarantee from another family member should not detract from this basic fact: had she counted for nothing, they could just as easily have sent her packing.

In seeking to heal Joseph Peters, the elders / initiators were undertaking an action that was bound to have an impact beyond one man. If the initiation succeeded, chances are good that balance would have been re-established in the Peters / Michaels relationship; stronger links would have been built between Peters and Michaels on the one hand, and the Salish community on the other; in so doing, a larger, healthier community would have been produced. The needs of Pat Michaels, at the very least, would have been met, and seeing her husband more integrated into the community would have served as a degree of insurance against the same problems reappearing at a later date. In that perspective it would seem that, at least in the practical outcome of actions, women such as Pat Michaels are included in the Coast Salish conception of "the community," the balance of which is to be maintained or re-established.

• • •

In the whitestream Peters/Michaels narrative, the imbalance between our concern for him and her invisibility makes the actions of the initiators appear almost unmotivated. The narrative gap feeds whitestream notions of savagery among natives; this is a shining example of the intertwining of "race" and gender in the colonial enterprise. That is to say, the positioning of native women in colonial discourse contributes to the destructuring of the colonized's culture and society. In this case, the mechanism of oppression in *Peters v. Campbell* combines race and gender in that the Court and media are able to narrate the superiority of Western culture (in its concern for individual rights) because they can/must push the concerns of Pat Michaels outside the frame of narrative relevance. And they are able to dismiss Pat Michaels because of the pre-established authority of the white stream over aboriginal peoples. Colonialism is reinforced through the erasure of women, at the same time that gender oppression is bolstered by whitestream cultural authority.

The interaction between gender oppression and colonialism has been little studied until recently, and as such their mutual reinforcement in this case may come as a surprise. In the last few years, however, the literature of postcolonialism has problematized the relationship, which is not so simple as to speak of the double oppression of women.[4] What is involved, among other things, is the strategic positioning of native women in / by the colonial apparatus such that they are made to destructure their communities.

---

4   See, in particular, Parker et. al (1992). Also Young (1995) and Ashcroft, Griffiths and Tiffin (1995). In the latter, the chapters in Part VIII and chapters by Benita Parry, Kadiatu Kanneh, and Gillian Whitlock are of special interest. On colonized women as doubly oppressed, see Gayatri Chakravorty Spivak's canonical "Can the Subaltern Speak?", reproduced at length in Williams and Chrisman (1994); a shorter excerpt, along with a critique by Benita Parry, is also found in Ashcroft, Griffiths and Tiffin (1995).

The connection between the two oppressions in the Peters / Michaels story is neither accidental nor unusual. It is, rather, an instance in the structuring of the social process of political community. That is to say, no political community exists without a membership and the criteria that define inclusion and exclusion, producing patterns of citizenship. The right to vote often serves as the key marker for citizenship, but it is not its sole component; other classical elements have been the ability to hold office, serve in the military, marry, work, own property, make a will (Guy, 1992). And grounds for (partial or total) exclusion from the political community in Canada as elsewhere have been gender as well as "race," resulting for instance in restrictions on the right to vote and to own property.

Exclusion and, in the case of aboriginal cultures, destructuring and assimilation being the goals of public policy, it is only to be expected that one ground for exclusion would bolster, sometimes reshape, the other and vice versa. As Andrew Parker and his co-editors of *Nationalisms and Sexualities* have written, "various colonialisms and postcolonialisms have altered consolidations of national and sexual identities" (1992: 9). Thus, the political theory embodied in the *Indian Act* held that persons endowed with Indian status had a special relationship with the Canadian state such that they were outside the Canadian political community – and this articulation of Indian status and political community was highly dependent on a person's gender.

Assimilation being the goal of policy, an aboriginal man was given the option of transferring to the Canadian political community by voting, an action that carried the automatic consequence of losing Indian status, of being "enfranchised."[5] And an aboriginal woman transferred from one community to the other by marrying a white man, the latter being the full rights-bearing subject of the Canadian political community. By losing her "Indian" status, she also lost among other things her right to reside on the reserve, to own property on the reserve, and to inherit property on the reserve (Weaver, 1993).

In this sense, it should be remembered that "ordinary" Canadian women along with status "Indians" of both sexes did not have the right to vote when, in 1869, the *Indian Act* removed status from aboriginal women (and their children) who married white men. For aboriginal women, straightforward double oppression came into play as long as white women did not acquire the right to vote in the years 1916-22.[6] Until then, aboriginal women who married white men lost the (dubious) advantages of status

5   This is a particularly perverse term to apply to this process of gaining the franchise in the Canadian political community by virtue of losing membership in the Canadian-defined "Indian" community.

6   Women in the three prairie provinces were the first to acquire the provincial franchise, in 1916; the federal franchise came in 1917. By 1922 all provinces but Quebec had granted women the right to vote. For Quebec women, it came in 1940. See Errington (1993).

without acquiring full membership in the dominant political community. Status-losing aboriginal women later acquired the right to vote before status Indians of both sexes did: after World War II provincially and in 1960 federally (Frideres, 1988). But irrespective of the right to vote and other features of membership in the dominant political community, aboriginal women marrying white men automatically acquired a role of destructuring the native community. This was not the case of aboriginal men marrying white women.

We have here a third oppression: not only are they dispossessed as women and as native, but as native women they are made agents of native destruction. One effect of this is that while an aboriginal man who married a white woman may have encountered some (or a lot of) disapproval in that he was bringing a dominant outsider into the community, an aboriginal woman who married a white man was likely to encounter much worse because she was taking herself and her children out, presumably forever. More broadly, women were given the job by the *Indian Act* of undermining the community's ability to maintain itself materially and culturally.

Practically, this vocation stemmed from the combination of two government policies: on the one hand, the goal of assimilating "Indians" by turning them into farmers and, on the other, the practice of conceiving of men as the head of the family. This latter policy was, of course, consistent with the practice across whitestream countries of having a woman's citizenship determined by her husband's (Guy, 1992). In that context, the government's colonialist theory held that if white men were allowed to control land on reserves, Indian farming (and therefore assimilation) would be undermined; the only way to keep the white husbands of aboriginal women from doing just that was to strip their wives of their status in the "Indian" community (see Weaver, 1993). It goes without saying that government did not consider white wives on reserves to be a corresponding threat. The fact that government consistently undermined the ability of "Indian" farmers to succeed at their new occupation (see Carter, 1990) only compounds the outrage to aboriginal women: not only were thousands of women cast out in the name of the policy of assimilation, but the community was impoverished by being denied real access to the supposed means of assimilation.[7]

Aboriginal women, then, lost the role they have claimed as the protectors and reproducers of culture, and were cast as the culture's enemy. It would have been surprising for this colonizing process to have no effect on gender relations among aboriginal women and men. Although traditional aboriginal culture is often presented as strongly favourable to women, the

---

7 It is far from clear that successful "Indian" farmers would have been assimilated as a result of their success — government theories can easily be well off the mark. Successful farmers would, in fact, have been able to contribute mightily to healthy communities. Impoverishment, for its part, brought massive social and cultural destruction on the reserves, but not much assimilation.

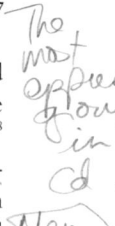

facts of life for aboriginal women are that they are surely the most oppressed group in contemporary Canada. And they are victims of, among others, the men in their communities – in what Lee Maracle calls "lateral violence."[8] The point is that nothing suggests that aboriginal culture as such is oppressive of women. It is quite possible that the oppression of aboriginal women stems entirely from colonialism's combination of gender and cultural oppression. A hint of all this is offered in the marginalization and humiliation of women in the *Peters v. Campbell* affair.

Thus, one general mechanism of gendered colonial oppression is regulation through marriage; for aboriginal women, Indian status has been a function of marriage in the context of whitestream assimilationist strategy (see Frideres, 1988 and Weaver, 1993). So it is that, in the Peters / Michaels story, it is through the marital relationship of Peters and Michaels (alluded to by the Judge calling her Mrs. Peters) that the destructuring of the Coast Salish community occurs. But here, the colonial use of marriage is reversed: it is by making the circumstances of "Mrs. Peters" irrelevant to the proceedings, and considering Mr. Peters strictly as a stand-alone Canadian citizen, that the Court undermines Coast Salish survival / development. Conversely, the elders / initiators honoured the marital relationship between two individuals whom they considered members of their community, by acting upon Michaels's request (as guaranteed by Peters's brother).

The role of this reversal of gender relations in the colonial enterprise is an important and revealing illustration of the discursive mechanism of oppression: gender relations will be discursively articulated in whatever ways are useful to the colonial enterprise, according to what the situation requires. Consistency based on universal principles – the hallmark of modernity's discourses of rights and the rule of law – has nothing to do with it.

● ● ●

The discursive mobility of the marital relationship in the colonial enterprise is an important example because of the controversy surrounding gender relations in aboriginal communities regarding self-government and the Canadian Charter of Rights and Freedoms. There may indeed be a lesson in the Peters / Michaels story, in light of the demand by aboriginal women's groups such as the Native Women's Association of Canada (NWAC), that self-government be subject to the Charter. Of the prospect of self-government, Winnie Giesbrecht, president of the Indigenous Women's Collective of Manitoba (IWCM), claimed: "My biggest fear is that native women are not

---

8 Lateral violence is "the violence of men and women against children and the violence of men toward women" (Maracle, 1996: ix). It is "about our anti-colonial rage working itself out in an expression of hate for one another" (11).

going to have any rights whatsoever. They will be controlled by the male powers in the native hierarchy."[9]

One can easily imagine that this fear is well founded for some communities and that for some others it is not. There is no doubt that attempts by aboriginal women to combat the sexism of the *Indian Act* over the past thirty years have met with stiff resistance from the leading First Nations organizations and from numerous bands (see Weaver, 1993). The question of whether the Charter might be an appropriate remedy against male control, however, is quite distinct from this problem. This latter question is very much within the ambit of the issues raised by the Peters / Michaels affair, but the previous one (of the extent to which communities across the country are male-controlled and indifferent to gender equality) is far outside the scope of this book.

Here is a woman, Pat Michaels, who asks for and obtains her aboriginal community's help in her relationship with her partner, only to find that a Canadian court disallows that help on the grounds of the common law, which is consistent with Charter values. In this case, the application of whitestream legal rights, far from favouring gender equality among aboriginal people, marginalizes the women involved at the same time that it reaffirms colonial rule. Does this story allow for generalization to the overall relationship between the Charter and aboriginal peoples? Or to the overall situation of women in First Nations communities? Does it help answer the question of whether self-government should be subject to the Charter?

If one takes seriously the claim to inherent self-government, the first thing to say is that First Nations should decide for themselves whether or not they *want* the Charter. They should not, in particular, be strong-armed into accepting Charter oversight in order to reach agreement on other issues. The question can then be reformulated: should First Nations want the Charter? Could First Nations women count on the Charter to advance gender equality?

Aboriginal critics of the pro-Charter argument have noted that the problems of aboriginal women are not of a kind that would be ameliorated by Charter oversight of self-government. What, after all, can legal rights do concretely for battered women, for sexually abused women, for women pushed into prostitution, etc.? Surely, the story of Pat Michaels speaks to this critique: faced with serious difficulties in her marital relationship, she found her attempt at dealing with them delegitimized in the name of legal rights consistent with the Charter – and it took two years for the Court to come to that decision, well after she and Joseph Peters had terminated the relationship. The almost immediate action taken by the elders of the Longhouse in response to her call for help looks all the better in contrast. The fact that

---

9   Winnie Giesbrecht, quoted in E. Kaye Fulton, "Drumbeats of Rage," *Maclean's*, 16 March 1992: 17.

there may have been resources in the whitestream community towards which Michaels could have turned instead does nothing to advance a pro-Charter argument; such resources were likely to have no direct relation to the Charter.

But the concerns of those who make the pro-Charter argument have to do with the specifically political empowerment of women, as opposed to their everyday living conditions and, in particular, the "lateral violence" which they endure. Without Charter oversight, they claim, the collective affairs of the community would be monopolized by men, who would be little concerned with the needs of women. This is more complicated, and of course Pat Michaels was anything but empowered as a result of her encounter with the Court. So it is clear that whitestream rights can be used against aboriginal women.

More generally, the concern expressed in pro-Charter arguments is grounded in the recent history of Bill C-31 which shows that the use of rights discourse in favour of aboriginal women can easily cut both ways. Once the Charter was adopted in 1982, all federal and provincial legislation was given three years to be brought into compliance with the new human rights code. In addition, at constitutional conferences on aboriginal rights held from 1983 on, the Charter's gender equality protection pushed participants towards amending the *Indian Act*: Bill C-31, *An Act to Amend the Indian Act*, was adopted in 1985 to harmonize the *Indian Act* with the Charter,[10] especially with regard to the sexual discrimination involved in women's loss of Indian status when marrying a non-Indian. While developed in specific response to Charter requirements, Bill C-31 also followed a three-decade long political and legal battle by aboriginal women to end the *Indian Act*'s sexism. During this time leading aboriginal organizations often stood in favour of the status quo, which goes a long way towards explaining the subsequent concerns of NWAC and IWCM over male-dominated organizations.[11]

One key aspect of Bill C-31 is that its application is retroactive: women who lost their status, and their children who never had it, could (re)gain it by applying to the Department of Indian Affairs. In the first year of Bill C-31's implementation, nearly 42,000 people applied for reinstatement (Frideres, 1988); by June 1990, registration applications for 133,134 people

---

10 Section 35(4) of the constitution also comes into play, linking specifically aboriginal rights and gender equality. This subsection, however, was adopted on the basis of the Charter and its ideology. In the account that follows, I will consequently focus on the Charter rather than on other legal / constitutional requirements.

11 For a detailed account of the political and legal process that preceded and followed the adoption of Bill C-31, see Weaver (1993) and Burrows (1997). For the complexities of the *Act*, including the multiplication of categories of "Indians" which it introduces, see also Frideres (1988: 10-11) and Joseph (1993), the latter providing a biting critique of the *Act* as a colonizing instrument. For personal testimony of the demeaning impact of the *Act*, see Mercredi (1993).

had been received by the Department (Joseph, 1993). But while status is returned by the federal government, it is local bands that have the responsibility to integrate new members. Bill C-31 introduced a distinction between Indian status and band membership, with procedures for the gradual incorporation of newly registered "Indians" into bands. While individual bands normally control their membership, the granting of status by the federal government puts pressure on bands to follow suit. Bands thereby lose a degree of their decision-making abilities, at the same time that they see increased population and economic pressures upon reserves that were already unable to ensure minimal social and economic development.

As many bands resented bitterly the federal government's further undermining of their autonomy and economic base, reinstated women have found themselves caught in the middle. Worse, while the federal government made itself look good by proclaiming loudly the end of sexual discrimination, it created a situation where bands were pushed into resisting the reinstatement of thousands of women – an institutional form of "lateral violence", furthering concerns about male-dominated band councils. But it is the federal government's legal construction of the situation, for the sake of compliance with the Charter, that has energized this tension between women and bands (on this conflict, see Burrows, 1997).

It is hard, in this context, to avoid the conclusion expressed by Shirley Joseph: "In reality, Bill C-31 has proven to be a modernized and more sophisticated instrument for the advancement of the age-old crusade of government to assimilate Indian people into Euro-Canadian society" (Joseph, 1993: 66). Bill C-31 was drafted and adopted because of Charter ideology, and was supposed to empower women. It ended up undermining aboriginal communities and placing thousands of women in an adversarial position toward the bands they were seeking to join. As the earlier gender discrimination had done, this Charter-driven development in government policy has weakened First Nations communities through antagonized gender relations.

● ● ●

It would be easy, at this point, to close the book on the Charter and whitestream rights in general, concluding that they are as inherently inimical to aboriginal women as "traditional" resources are helpful. Certainly, we have seen how rights discourse often works against oppressed groups even when its proponents claim that it helps them. Indeed, research on the Charter shows that it has helped dominant interests consolidate their position at least as much as it has furthered the empowerment of subordinate groups.[12]

---

12 See for instance Mandel (1994) and Bakan (1991).

Conversely, the willingness of Longhouse members to decisively help Pat Michaels, along with numerous accounts of the honoured role of women in aboriginal cultures across North America, point to the potential of aboriginal resources to redress the situation of women. This diagnosis would seem to be confirmed by an article published in *The Regional News* a few weeks after the *Peters v. Campbell* decision, profiling a women's shelter on one of the reserves near Islandtown. This shelter, run by aboriginal women, was helping "hundreds of women and children" every year (RN 8). Such a shelter could not, of course, be considered a traditional aboriginal resource: the model is that of institutions established by whitestream women's organizations in the context of second-wave feminism. It deals, also, with problems that have clearly developed in the context of the colonial oppression of aboriginal peoples. But it is run by aboriginal women, for aboriginal women, on uncontested "Indian land." Surely, this would make it an aboriginal resource – a part of the cultural project of aboriginality dynamically seeking to escape colonialism.

The situation, however, is complicated; it is not so simple as trashing the Charter and hailing aboriginality. The difficulty has to do with the relationship between grand narratives and everyday life. This relationship, as I have tried to show, is undetermined in principle. Circumstances and context will bind grand narratives to various practices in the interplay of social power.

An interesting example of this is provided by Joanne Pelkey, the aunt of Joseph Peters. Asked what effect the whole affair of her nephew's initiation had on her family, Ms Pelkey, herself a member of the Longhouse, testified that "it was not too much, that she stayed at home most of the time, and did not really associate with the family" (146; this is Judge Hood's paraphrase of the testimony.). It could also be, of course, that she did not want to find herself in conflict with her nephew. Either way, her distance from her nephew's troubles is something of a rebuke to Lara Skye's claim in *The Globe and Mail* that the case could be properly understood only by starting from the notion that, in aboriginal life, "the family is responsible for the welfare of its members." As a lawyer involved in the defence of traditionalist aboriginal practices, she could be expected to situate her case within such a discourse.

A proper scepticism toward grand narratives would generally be good preparation for the discrepancy between Ms Pelkey's conduct and Lara Skye's claim: official value systems and the everyday life of ordinary people are often at considerable variance with each other. That aboriginal peoples are not immune to this tendency should not be surprising, but considerations of discursive politics often work to steer analysis away from such tensions, for fear of delegitimizing aboriginal claims.

In this perspective, we have to consider that not only have women encountered strong resistance from male aboriginal leaders in addressing the sexism of the *Indian Act*, but, more generally, aboriginal resources do not exist in a vacuum. They operate in the context of impoverished reserves and urban communities, along with various forms of interference from the federal and provincial governments. Thus, while the aboriginal women's shelter portrayed in *The Regional News* seemed to have acquired a valued role among the women of the community, the same cannot be said of all such projects.

The "South Vancouver Island Justice Project" is a good example of some difficulties encountered.[13] Established as a way to divert aboriginal offenders from the whitestream justice system and toward their communities, it backfired badly; distrust of the actual conduct of the project was such that in 1992 the Naukana Native Women's Association, representing "Saanich Peninsula native victims of violence and abuse," was founded to fight it. The Naukana Association quickly gained the support of several other organizations, including the Native Council of Canada. As reported in *The Victoria Times-Colonist*, the problems of the South Island project included "revelations ... of intimidation and fear on the Peninsula reserves at the hands of powerful leaders, elders and families in positions to prevent disclosures by victims." Women in the communities were reportedly "outraged that aboriginal male sex offenders are roaming free of punishment in aboriginal communities after being charged or convicted for violent offences against women and children." And they were "concerned that the Coast Salish bighouse, traditionally a place of spiritual initiation and honor, is being used to 'heal' offenders" (Nathan, 1993: A1).

Although we have seen that "spiritual initiation" can indeed be considered a form of "healing", there is no question that a good part of the community in the reserves involved in the South Island project felt that justice was not being done. In the Michaels / Peters situation, spiritual healing was brought into the picture at the request of the woman seeking help; in the South Island project, a number of women thought that similar practices were used to get men off the hook, as a result of the influence of some in the community.

In the controversy over the South Island Project, claims were made that the whole community had not been brought in the planning and conduct of the project, and that if this was done the problems would go away. It is not clear that this rhetoric of consensus, which is as characteristic of aboriginal identities as the rhetoric of rights is typical of whitestream identities, would be adequate to the task of, for example, curbing the influence of some families or individuals. It is in this sceptical perspective that, in this book's Introduction, I suggested that social power is not abolished among the Indians. Powerful individuals, families, and groups will often make use

---

13 This account is based on Nathan (1993).

of whatever resources (discursive and otherwise) are available to maintain and enhance their positions. I would want to suggest that subordinate individuals and groups need not deny themselves the same flexibility. Such a pragmatic approach would disqualify Charter worship as a desirable political stance.

Chapter 6
Pluralisms

◄───►

"By living this way, we cared for the Earth, for
our brothers and sisters in the animal world and for each other."
— OVIDE MERCREDI

There is no getting away from social power.

The women of the Naukana Association who challenged the South Island Justice Project (see Chapter 5) were outraged and concerned that certain individuals and families, backed by whitestream governments, were wielding their power to protect abusers of women and children. In calling for a halt, review, and audit of the program, the Naukana Association women claimed that they were seeking the disappearance of social power. We may better understand their enterprise as aiming towards a redeployment of social power in conformity with their interests and needs.

It is something like that which Pat Michaels got from the Long House elders. Unable on her own to achieve a resolution of her marital problems, she reached for the power of the men and women of the Long House. And Joseph Peters found himself the unhappy object of their wielding of social power. In both cases, there was bound to be an unhappy party, although it was possible that Peters could have emerged from the process of his initiation reborn, as it were, and "healed."

This is a different issue from that of justice. A particular exercise of social power may or may not be considered just within a given regime of power; the same practice may have a wholly different status in another. And in judging whether a particular practice is just and legitimate, it often does not matter that the targeted individual(s) may protest; think of imprisoned criminals, for instance, or of recalcitrant children disciplined by their parents. Not that such cases are entirely unproblematic; equating justice with the legal process is not only debatable in principle (see for instance Cornell, 1992), it is also an obnoxious notion in matters such as those at the heart of this book. As well, establishing what (if anything) would be the proper authority of parents over children is not a simple thing. The point here is that in contemporary Canadian society, as in many others, the exercise of social power through such things as the courts, or parental authority, is widely considered legitimate.

What we have in the *Peters v. Campbell* case and the South Island Justice Project controversy, however, are challenges to the legitimacy of various regimes of power. And these challenges would redeploy, rather than neutralize, social power, Peters toward the reaffirmation of the Canadian state's authority over aboriginal peoples, and the Naukana Association toward greater autonomy for aboriginal communities and greater say for women.

Compared to the controversy over the South Island project, the situation of Joseph Peters was straightforward: he was identifying squarely with the Canadian state against aboriginal rights, and claiming that he knew little of Coast Salish culture and wanted nothing to do with the Longhouse. The Naukana Association, on the other hand, argued for greater aboriginal autonomy, in the process of attacking a project that bands and governments had created jointly with the declared purpose of increasing community control and enacting traditional practices of social control. As reported in *The Times-Colonist*, part of the Association's concern was that the project "reflects values that the community does not support ... They charge that cultural and racial considerations mitigate sentencing of aboriginal men convicted of violent sexual crimes against women and children" (Nathan, 1993). And, as already noted, they were not pleased with the Salish big house "being used to 'heal' offenders."

● ● ●

Such disagreements among aboriginal men and women are happening in a context of continued colonialism in the relationship between Canada and aboriginal peoples. How much of it would change after decolonization? It is first important to ask what should be expected: are "Indians" supposed to unanimously agree on a model of government? On its actual implementation? During the 1992 Charlottetown referendum process, when Canadians challenged First Nations leaders to "deliver" their communities' vote and provide a detailed definition of self-government that would apply across the country, they replied: if whitestream Canadians are able to disagree among themselves on political issues, why should aboriginal people be of one mind? There was, in fact, widespread disagreement with the Charlottetown Accord among aboriginal communities, leading to many boycotts of the vote on reserves.

Looking at internal dynamics of aboriginal communities such as those narrated here, anyone harbouring Edenic illusions about harmony among "the Indians" ought to rethink that notion. Something that should be obvious, were it not for the ideological overdetermination of discourse on aboriginal-whitestream relations, does indeed become apparent: individual persons, no matter what their culture, think for themselves, come to their own conclusions (in terms allowed by their cultural context) and are likely to dis/agree with their neighbour(s) on a variety of issues regarding their lives.

Members of aboriginal peoples in Canada are living in a markedly pluralist cultural context, which makes available to them any number of discursive possibilities with respect to such issues as government and spirituality. Thus, not only are they forced to reckon with the band system imposed by the Canadian government, but they are presented with a variety of traditionalist models of self-government, not to mention all manner of government as can be found across the globe. As well, while traditional spirituality is a strong component in the current self-affirmation of aboriginal communities, many of their members continue to identify with a large number of Christian churches. As well, there is nothing to keep them from drawing parallels with, and learning from, Asian philosophies, as Ovide Mercredi and others have been doing.[1]

It should be expected that individual members of aboriginal communities will be found all over the spectrum of possibilities. And these do not merely include options predefined by past and current experience, but also large numbers of hybrid compromises that are likely to improve on anyone of the initial choices. These, in turn, are not pristine expressions (whatever that might be) of separate cultures, but rather are the result of decades and centuries of interaction between/among aboriginal peoples and the white stream. For it is a constant of life in society that we do not merely repeat what is given us. Presented with an array of elements that, taken as a whole, is always unprecedented, we pick and choose among them, fabricating combinations that will participate in shaping our futures.

The situation out of which the Naukana Association was founded is at once an odd hybrid and a typical example of the dilemmas faced by aboriginal peoples in Canada and elsewhere: whitestream state involvement, under the guise of liberal democracy, articulated with partial aboriginal control and traditional discourse, fosters conflict and controversy within native communities. In and around these communities, a whole spectrum of opinion can indeed be found among members of aboriginal peoples, going from a thoroughgoing identification with the Canadian state, *à la* Joseph Peters, to proponents of forms of self-government that go from a municipal model to full statehood. Further, as the South Island project shows, autonomist and traditionalist discourse can be articulated by individuals and groups in conflict, each accusing the other of such things as bad faith, selfishness, treason, and so on.

● ● ●

---

1 See for instance the parallels drawn by J. Couture (1991) between aboriginal and other forms of mysticism. On Mercredi's learning from the teachings of the Mahatma Gandhi, see his book *In the Rapids* (1993: 53-8); and Murray Campbell, "Selling a philosophy of peace in Indian Country," *The Globe and Mail*, 2 March 1996, D1.

There is no getting away from social conflict. More specifically, I should say, there is no getting away from social conflict in matters of life in society and of government. Matters of spirituality are a (partly) different story, to which we will return in the next chapter.

In the current situation of Canadian colonialism over aboriginal peoples, some aboriginal women and men take the view that "traditional forms of government" may no longer be appropriate and can be supplemented or replaced by whitestream-influenced processes and institutions. Further, this can be done in the context of municipal-type government, within the Canadian state as currently constituted, although they add that of course the *Indian Act* remains grievously injurious and should be removed (see for instance Jeffries, 1993). The 1996 agreement between the federal and BC governments and the Nisga'a nation fits that description to a considerable extent, while establishing also large elements of "traditional" government involving such things as collective decision-making and membership criteria. But, as noted in Chapter 1, much more radical models are put forward by pan-Canadian organizations and individual nations, whether on the Prairies or Iroquois territory. Most radically, some aboriginal writers condemn the bulk of the "Native elite" in its efforts at negotiating with Canada's governments. Thus, self-described rebel writer Lee Maracle claims that "(t)he Native elite ... owes both its existence and its loyalty to the piper that paid it to play the tune," the piper being the Canadian government (1996: 37-8).

Whatever process leads to self-governing aboriginal nations across Canada, these controversies among aboriginal men and women will remain: aboriginal people are people too, not angels. Struggles for influence, discursive and otherwise, will continue to be part and parcel of the aboriginal communities' process of defining how they want to govern themselves and then, indeed, of how they actually do govern themselves.

All involved in matters of aboriginal government will surely claim to articulate a vision culturally appropriate to their people, and many will challenge their adversaries' claim. All will also carry a variety of whitestream influences that shape parts of their vision. This latter fact is recognized even by Lee Maracle, in her reluctant admission that she is indeed an intellectual despite her deeply felt aversion for this social role emerging out of whitestream society and making her, somehow, a member of that elite which she so despises.

Now, who is to arbitrate between competing claims to a culturally appropriate form of self-government? Absent divine intervention recognized by all, pointing to an actually correct model, no one is in a disengaged position to provide a final word on what is appropriate and what is not. There is no getting out, then, of what the white stream calls the political process of debating claims and convincing constituencies of the goodness of one's model rather than that of an adversary.

Political pluralism, in other words, is a fact of today's and tomorrow's life among aboriginal peoples and not merely in terms of who gets to be a leader with what agenda, but also in fundamental terms of defining the norms governing the community's collective life.

• • •

As is the case in whitestream societies, the political accommodation of religious / spiritual pluralism will be a crucial test for freedom in aboriginal communities.

In arguing that he wanted to be treated as an ordinary Canadian citizen, Joseph Peters sought to opt out not only of an aboriginal political process, but also of an aboriginal spirituality, the two of them combining in a repudiation of liberal modernity's ideological insistence on the separation of church and state. In whitestream societies, the boundaries of what is considered political have widened in the past few decades, as new social movements have put into question the legitimacy of the existing social order (see for instance Habermas, 1975; and Maier, 1987). In this connection, just as earlier we worked on the notion of "cruelty" (Chapter 3), we must now look at "the political." The general point is that what counts as political is not always and everywhere the same.

In their specific processes of development, societies decide for themselves what use, if any, they have for an explicitly political field, separate from others such as the religious or spiritual. It is often said, in this perspective, that "the Greeks and Romans invented politics" (Finley, 1983: 54) and, indeed, the word politics is derived from the Greek word *polis*, meaning city. The discursive instability of "the political" is seen most evidently in the fact that the word politics is understood differently in various languages: in French, for example, *politique* includes the meanings of the English words *politics* and *policy*. And if this is variable, it must be that the positioning of "the spiritual" in relation to "the political" will also vary. Indeed, and most importantly for us, not every society in world history has had a concept of the political as separate from other spheres of life and, in particular, from spiritual concerns.

As Aristotle's *Politics* shows, the Greeks, and especially the citizens of the Athenian city-state, established a sense of the political that remains the basis of what Western societies understand as politics. Aristotle's *polis* is defined by the freedom and equality of its members, to the exclusion of inferior non-members (women and slaves, not to mention animals), and by the debatable character of government among equals. Relationships between unequals are not to be debated; by definition, these are outside the political field – they are natural, in the order of things.

This remains the dynamic that sees social movements trying to widen the range of what can count as a debatable issue, as opposed to the kind of thing that is natural, and therefore not debatable. From the women's movement that has turned violence against women into a political issue out of what was considered a private matter to the aboriginal movement that has challenged the "natural" superiority of white civilization and the inevitability (and virtue) of assimilation, politics expands, or shrinks, as a function of social struggles. Indeed, the emergence of something called politics has been one way to express, to speak social struggles. But it is not the only one. If politics had to be invented (by the Romans and Greeks), it is because at certain places and times, societies go about their business without politics – which does not mean, of course, without conflict. And, unless one takes an evolutionary view, there is no reason to think that the institution of a separate political sphere is the best way for a society to process its conflicts.[2] This is an important thing to keep in mind as we approach our discussion of the relationship between politics and spirituality.

Islamic discourse, for example, links spiritual and worldly power very closely, in a way that is explicitly in contradiction with Western ideas of the separation of church and state. At the birth of Islam in the seventh century AD, Muhammad was accepted as a prophet by his followers in the same process that he became the ruler of the city of Medina, and then of an ever-expanding empire. His successors, the *khalifa*, inherited this position of religious and community leadership: "the caliphate possessed three elements: that of legitimate succession to the Prophet, that of directing the affairs of the world and that of watching over the faith" (Hourani, 1991: 143).[3]

One reason why it is important for us to note Islam's difference with Western modernity in this respect is that, at the end of the twentieth century, after the collapse of Soviet communism, it is one of the few models with the ability to mobilize millions of people against the inequities of a large number of societies. Some writers go so far as to say that "it may be possible to argue that ... Islam can now function as the major alternative, perhaps even the only alternative to Western capitalist hegemony" (Turner, 1994: 12).

The combination of the political and the spiritual in Islam is generally seen by Westerners as dangerous for democracy and pluralism, Islamic

---

2 This is just what such modernists as Habermas, his followers, and fellow-travellers do, however: arguing that the differenciation of spheres is an achievement of the Enlightenment, they claim that it must be preserved and strengthened if we are to avoid falling back into more primitive and oppressive types of social systems. See for instance Habermas (1987).

3 I should add, as Hourani himself shows, and to discourage misunderstandings, that the theological merging of secular and religious power in Islam has not been consistently (or even often) realized in the practice of Muslim societies. My point is that, ideologically, Islam and the West are at polar opposites in constructing the relationship between church and state. We will see below that Western societies fail to live up to their own ideological standard in keeping religion out of politics.

regimes such as Iran's and Saudi Arabia's providing much ammunition to that view. But no matter what one thinks of Islam's democratic and pluralist capabilities,[4] it would be a mistake to think it the only alternative to Western capitalism and modernity, either as a model or adversary, or in terms of its global reach: the indigenous peoples of the Americas and of Australasia can also offer models, and ought to be considered a global player. This is forcefully argued in Jerry Mander's *In the Absence of the Sacred* (1991), which makes the case that "the native alternative" should be seen as the alternative to modernity's ever increasing and destructive valuing of "megatechnology."[5]

The small size of indigenous populations in Canada, the United States, Australia, and New Zealand in proportion to whitestream populations contributes to a natural (that is, colonial) tendency among members of the white stream to look at them as perhaps interesting and clearly exotic, but surely marginal. But indigenous populations are in much greater numbers in other parts of their continents. The whitestream tendency to marginalize ought to be resisted, then, not only on moral and political grounds, but also on material grounds. Globally, indigenous peoples are a big player. Surely, their experience(s) of the political/spiritual separation is (are) as weighty as those of Islam and modernity.

But numbers are not all that counts. Thus, in the Report of the Royal Commission on Aboriginal Peoples one can read an echo of Mander's claims for "the native alternative":

> We became convinced that distinctively Aboriginal ways of apprehending reality and governing collective and individual behaviour are relevant to the demands of survival in a post-industrial society. And we concluded that this heritage must be made more accessible to all Canadians. (Canada, 1996A: 616)

This goal is all the more important that, as the Report notes, "... the Aboriginal vision of their future is one that easily accommodates new relationships and new elements of culture" (Canada, 1996A: 620). It is not just about making sense of past errors and injustices, in other words, that the aboriginal vision shows alternative ways of knowing. It is a dynamic vision,

---

4   Need I add that the issue is not as cut and dried as the condemnation of the Iranian regime would have one believe? In addition to Hourani (1991) and Turner (1994), see, of course, Said (1978) and the debate around his *Orientalism*; for instance the chapters by Aijaz Ahmad and Dennis Porter in Williams and Chrisman (1994). On the media construction of the Islamic other, see Said (1981).

5   Mander writes that it is precisely because it is the alternative that aboriginality has been and remains the target of massive eliminationist efforts across the globe.

capable of taking in the whole of contemporary experience in all of its inter-cultural complexity.[6]

Thirty years ago, members of the white stream would have received Ovide Mercredi's description of what aboriginal self-government had con-sisted of in the centuries before European contact (see Chapter 4) as, at best, quaint. If he had been heard at all, images of Jean-Jacques Rousseau's *bon sauvage* might have come to mind, along perhaps with a vaguely sentimen-tal thought to Francis of Assisi's poem to "Brother Sun."[7]

Certainly, the job of government was not seen as caring for the Earth and our animal relatives. This is still not what governments do today, but the environment and animal rights are squarely on the political agenda: large numbers of people in most Western countries want government to concern itself with these issues. The ethos advocated by First Nations does not seem so quaint or outdated anymore, and this surely accounts for part of the sym-pathy that the aboriginal struggle has elicited recently in many countries.[8] But one cannot say that this ethos has quite been taken seriously yet, in terms of its complexity and the radicality of the challenge it presents to the modern description of the world. One aspect of that challenge is its invita-tion to reconsider our attitude to the political and its relationship to spiritu-ality.

Connections with Eastern philosophy should be made, in this respect as in others (see note 1 above). While whitestream intellectuals often see Buddhism (among other outlooks) as bolstering conservative social orders, it is in fact the case today that Buddhists all over Asia have made it an impor-tant political force working for various forms of democracy (including among aboriginal peoples of that region).[9] Beyond Asia, a consideration of Buddhist philosophy can contribute to attempts such as Chantal Mouffe's at articulating "groundless democracy" (see Horowitz, 1992).

● ● ●

Along with the emphasis on the avoidance of cruelty, the separation of church and state is a key component of liberal thinking. Put in a more tech-

---

6 On this issue of aboriginal takes on inter- or multiculturalism, see R.A. Williams (1994) who shows how the Iroquois Confederacy at the time of the encounter with Europe had already developed sophisticated ways of dealing with their own multicultural situation.

7 For many, this latter connection might have become visible only with the 1973 film of St. Francis by Franco Zeffirelli, *Brother Sun, Sister Moon.*

8 However, the green and animal rights movements on one hand and the aboriginal movement on the other have had their conflicts. The former's campaign for banning fur obtained from trapped animals has hurt aboriginal people in northern Canada, many of whom rely on trap-ping for a living and claim it as an important element of their traditional way of life.

9 See, on this issue, the fascinating Queen and King (1996).

nical way, this separation is the requirement that moral ideas of right and wrong do not enter into law-making, except on the rare issues where different moral traditions hold overlapping positions.[10] This requirement is expressed canonically in the Constitution of the United States, which forbids government from discriminating against or favouring any religion. For liberalism, the importance of this principle stems from the fact of religious pluralism in our societies: if citizens with various religious beliefs are to be treated equally by government (which they should be), laws must be made on grounds that are not religious. In Canada recently, this principle as expressed in the Charter of Rights and Freedoms has led for instance to the repeal of "Lord's Day" laws that curtailed commercial activity on Sundays.[11]

Two things with regard to this principle of moral neutrality must be underlined here. First, although it is of paramount importance in liberal doctrine, this principle has been and remains very unevenly applied in such societies (and many more) as the United Kingdom, the United States, France, and Canada. Meanwhile, in all these countries, in the current context of extra-Christian religious pluralism, minorities can experience the quasi-secularism of public institutions as oppressive, as the RCMP turban controversy in Western Canada and the Islamic scarf controversies in France and Quebec have shown. Most recently, the controversy in Germany over the Church of Scientology has been a sharp reminder that the (liberal and democratic) German state has a privileged relationship with three religions to the detriment of all others.[12]

And *quasi*-secularism dies hard.

If, in Canada, "Lord's Day" laws had to be repealed recently, it is because they had been well entrenched for generations, while in several provinces

---

10 There is a large debate within liberalism and between liberals and others on this issue. I just want to note here that even "procedural" liberals such as John Rawls and Ronald Dworkin accept that in order to be generally neutral, one has to make a prior moral commitment to pluralism and democracy; it is only given such a prior commitment that it is possible to establish neutral rules based on the imperative of allowing individuals to make their own, unimpeded, moral decisions on "the good life." Rawls (1993) came to this position from the more broadly neutral position of his *A Theory of Justice* (1972), which he and his critics eventually found unsustainable. And see Dworkin's new book, *Freedom's Law*, which although not yet available at this writing was excerpted in Dworkin (1996).

11 Some such laws have been upheld, however, on the grounds that their rationale has been "secularized." But having been secularized, they come out of particular religious traditions. These will be foreign to any number of people, who will justifiably see the link between past and present, and accordingly feel alienated. This outcome shows the "secularization" to be a fig leaf, hiding the shallowness of the separation of church and state.

12 These three religions are the Lutheran and Catholic churches, and Orthodox/Conservative Judaism. On the Scientology controversy and Germany's established churches, see Joffe (1997).

government-financed school systems remain at least partly denominational.[13] As well, a significant portion of the hard-right values animating the Reform Party, and even some Liberal members of Parliament, are explicitly religious.[14] In the UK, Anglicanism remains the established Church, with the Queen (and, one expects, the King one day soon) as head of the Church of England. Even if this changes soon, it will have been the case for the whole of the twentieth century, not to mention centuries before. In the United States, one of the most potent political forces today (perhaps the single most potent force) is the evangelical right, which has been a significant influence on public policy since the Reagan presidency and is growing in strength and influence (despite the Republican defeat in the 1996 presidential election).[15] It is in France that the separation principle has been most consistently applied since the end of the nineteenth century, with the exception of the Pétain years during World War II. But this is not because of a stronger French devotion to grand ideas: in the century-long political struggles following the 1789 revolution, the eventual winners were the anti-clerical republicans, and the losers were the Catholic monarchists; therefore, republican institutions such as the school became adamantly secular.

France's republican history of political struggle over religion points to the second thing that needs to be emphasized here: the political principle of moral neutrality acquired its importance in Western societies, and its even greater importance in Western philosophy and ideology, in the particular historical context of religious pluralism and war that came out of the Protestant Reformation (Cornell, 1992). The wars of religion that ravaged Europe for over a century, from the mid-1500s, led directly to the recognition of some religious toleration on the Continent starting with the 1648 Peace of Westphalia, and in the UK with the 1688 Glorious Revolution (Shklar, 1989). In the meantime, British colonists to North America, who had been traumatized by the religious wars, brought with them the distrust

13 The Supreme Court of Canada reaffirmed, in November 1996, the constitutionality of such denominational systems, allowing in particular the Ontario government to fund Catholic schools alongside public schools and to deny funding to other religious communities. At this writing, however, the United Nations Human Rights Committee is considering whether this system is in breach of internationally recognized human rights. See Virginia Galt, "Ontario not obligated to fund religious schools," *The Globe and Mail*, 22 November 1996, A1, A7.

14 See, for instance, the debate over the protection of gay rights in federal law. Along with the whole Reform Party caucus, four Liberal MPs were adamantly opposed to such protection, on religious grounds (see Joan Bryden, "Gay rights issue may prove explosive," *The Edmonton Journal*, 1 June 1995; and "Better to have a pregnant daughter than a gay one – MP," *The Edmonton Journal*, 21 December 1995). After a long battle, the federal government in the winter of 1996 withdrew its commitment to modify its human rights law.

15 Not to mention the quite devout President Carter's moral advocacy of human rights, and the debates that surrounded the election of John Kennedy as the first Catholic president.

of established Churches that eventually found its way in the US Constitution along with such things as the 8th Amendment's interdiction of cruel and unusual punishment (see Chapter 3, note 25).

Outside such a historical context of religious pluralism and war, the principle of separation of church and state loses much of its sheen. Far from being a principle with obvious universal validity, it is very much a historically specific artefact, one that stems not from European philosophical virtue, but rather from the horrors of European history. Other contexts – Coast Salish or Moorish Spain's religious toleration under Islamic predominance until 1492, to name but two – have produced other forms and languages of liberty.

This, in turn, means that the principle of church / state separation is not inherently necessary to individual freedom, contrary to what (even radical) liberal philosophers would have us believe (see Mouffe, 1994). Thus, they argue that for an individual to enjoy freedom, s/he must be free to choose *between* moral standards, without pressure from the law; between, say, the decision Catholicism, Anglicanism or atheism would have you make about an unhappy marriage (to divorce or not to divorce). But, clearly, individuals make moral choices *within* a religious or spiritual outlook, and in doing so they exercise freedom. In this sense, it is absurd to think that a situation without a plurality of religions precludes individual freedom. By the same token, it must be abusive to assume that the distinction church / state, religion / politics has to be available in a cultural vocabulary in order for individual freedom to be even thinkable.

Finally, it is far from clear that individuals choose moral standards. It is more the case that, as members of communities of meaning, individuals inhabit moral standards, are chosen by them. Thus, suppose that I explicitly choose to follow one or another moral path on an issue that is thrown in my way; on what basis do I make that choice? I have to rely on some more general or fundamental precept, which I am likely not articulating explicitly. This precept surely has competitors, among all of which I might have chosen at some point; on what basis did I make that prior choice? The chain is endless: presuppositions, pre-given choices, always come before willed decisions. It is in this sense that it can be said that each of us inhabits moral standards, within which we choose (on this deconstructive logic, see Fish, 1989).

•   •   •

What is the point of all this? Two things (again). First, modernity's banishment of spirituality from the public sphere is an historically contingent fact, to which it is not necessary for the whole of humanity to aspire. Second, politics (like cruelty) being a historically and culturally specific artefact, it is not necessarily helpful to think of the events surrounding the initiation of Joseph Peters in terms of strictly political issues. There is a third element that binds the political and spiritual aspects of this operation in historical contextualizing: the centralization of all public functions in "the state," placing politics at the centre of society, and spirituality at its edge or margin.

One of the striking aspects of the initiation of Joseph Peters is that it happened independently of a centralized band authority: it was the Longhouse that was called upon to help Peters, not the band; it was elders of the Longhouse who made the decision to proceed, not the band's chief. In the published accounts of the story (including the judgement), nothing indicates that the band had a problem with this process, either with the fact of the initiation itself, or with its going ahead without regard for band authority. It seems that this (at least) dual authority is something that was not immediately grasped by Joseph Peters's lawyer. He initiated the lawsuit not only against the individuals involved (including Pat Michaels), but also against the two bands some of whose members were the initiators. Significantly, the suit against the two bands (and Pat Michaels) was eventually dropped.

If one considers that Coast Salish authority structures, like those of many other First Nations, are partly clan-based, it is easy to see that a given community will be traversed by multiple centres of power, each partly autonomous from the others. As the authority of the Longhouse elders is partial, so are those of the chief, and of the clan mothers, etc.. Why not, in this connection, call the authority structure decentralized among (for instance) clan mothers, elders and chief, a system of checks and balances capable of protecting individuals from the accumulation of too much power into too few hands?

Shklar (1989: 37) has written that "the institutions of a pluralist order with multiple centres of power and institutionalized rights" are a characteristic of liberalism. We have seen in previous chapters that something like "rights" can be institutionalized in more ways than the whitestream one. Certainly, the first half of Shklar's characterization of liberalism fits the authority structure of any number of aboriginal cultures. What, then, remains so unique or outstanding about liberalism?

Thus, not only are there more ways than one of ensuring liberty, but the *Peters v. Campbell* case suggests that, in a variety of situations, liberalism is not necessarily the most effective way to reach this goal. Compare once again concrete micro-social practices with ideology, the actions undertaken by Longhouse members to actually help Pat Michaels with the grand narrative of Charter (and other whitestream) rights.

In a society with no state monopoly of public authority, with no church/state doctrine (and no need for one as long as there is no monopolizing state power), there are multiple centres of power, which can be quite fluid and which are more independent from each other than various branches of government will ever be. It is, in fact, the whole dichotomy between state and the "public" on the one hand, and civil society and the "private" on the other, that is destabilized in aboriginal communities: the separate authorities of clan mothers, chiefs, and elders can all be considered public, in that their exercise may reach all corners of the community, although at least some of them are private also, in the sense of being grounded in families.

It is the public/private dichotomy itself that becomes an inadequate means of understanding such authority structures: the individual is implicated in social relationships that engage at once public and private privileges and responsibilities. By the same token, in a situation where "the public" is institutionally diffuse, the relationship between governance and spirituality is bound to be figured in ways different from those of state-centered societies such as modern Canada.[16] Something like this can be recognized in the Report of the Royal Commission on Aboriginal Peoples' description[17] of aboriginal spirituality:

> Aboriginal spirituality therefore had both private and public dimensions. Responsibility for observing the requirements of natural and spiritual law rested with the individual, but misfortune in the family or the interdependent community was considered evidence of a failure of morality or an offended spirit. Setting the problem right was a concern of the whole community, and ceremonialists, medicine persons or shamans were the agents called upon to diagnose the problem and restore balance on behalf of the community. (Canada, 1996A: 629)

What if self-government were to be established with a form of centralized authority, doing away with such things as clan authorities and elders? This is highly unlikely to happen in a wholesale manner. But existing arrangements such as the Sechelt band's in British Columbia and the emerging Nisga'a model do establish forms of government that borrow significantly from the white stream. Still, the political organization of the Nisga'a accord is partly structured along clan lines, in which authority is understood as inherited; as well, it affirms a role for elders, who draw their authority from the development of wisdom. Such a system, in fact, combines forms of authority that draw their legitimacy from diverse sources and that accomplish different tasks. Thus, elders will be involved in the justice system's decision-making and they will advise elected leaders, who will ignore them at the peril of their own legitimacy.

---

16 For the theoretical underpinnings of this notion of "state-centered society," see Denis (1989).

17 This description presents aboriginal spirituality in the past tense in the context of that particular section of the Report, but it should be understood as applying to the present just as well, as an understanding of the Joseph Peters initiation makes plain.

The key characteristic of such decentralization, it turns out, is not so much a matter of concentration of power in a few or many hands. Rather, the heart of the matter is the diversity of sources of legitimacy through which social power is exercised. In whitestream modernity, we recognize only one source of legitimacy: the people, constituted as citizens of the state.[18] Given such a scheme, all other groupings are "voluntary associations," "interest groups," etc., all subject to the the ultimate authority of "the people" through state action.

Trying to apply this model to aboriginal communities is hopeless. We are going to misconstrue what we are witnessing, whether we are looking at reserves governed by the *Indian Act*, the Nisga'a accord or remembered communities as they are imagined and longed for by traditionalists. Consequently, when one considers the fact of religious / spiritual pluralism in aboriginal communities, the issue must be redefined: individuals and groups acting in the name of their faith may be able to act as a counterweight to others acting in the name of clan, for instance. They may do this, because their ability to do so is dependent on the legitimacy of that particular faith in the community. They are not, then, particularly vulnerable to an absolute / universal power of state. Rather, once they have succeeded in obtaining general recognition for their faith from the community as structured through its various power centres, they become one of its authorities in a situation of interdependence and tension with others, but not subject to ultimate state authority.

One might expect that a structure of authority decentralized in terms of institutions and foundations (such as the one described here) would feed conflict and competition – and what if it did? Superficially, this would seem to contradict the notion advanced by many exponents of aboriginal cultures, who insist on the importance of consensual decision-making in native traditions. But consensus has to be searched for, attained; community meetings may last hours and days until a consensus is indeed reached. What more does one need to see that consensus is not spontaneous, prior to discussion, and that large disagreements may exist at the outset? As well, rational discussion is not the only way to reach a consensus, and there is no reason to exclude the possibility that social influence and various forms of pressure will be brought to bear in the course of discussion, in order to produce agreement. Just this form of consensus-making is in fact pin-pointed as one of the sources of the Naukana Association's dissatisfaction with the South Island Justice Project.

Consensus does not exhaust social power. The issue is whether or not social power is articulated in democratic ways, and whether or not this artic-

---

18 In Canada, this sense of the people as sovereign is a recent constitutional development. But the polity has functioned on the basis of this principle for much longer. On this issue among others, the Constitution has had difficulty keeping up with actual political practice.

ulation is seen by community members to be legitimate. Aboriginal traditionalism, in this connection, articulates an ethos of discussion and debate in collective decision-making that would seem wholly compatible with ideals of democracy. Still, as Lee Maracle (1996: 37) reminds us, it could be that, within traditionalist discourse, a community's "elite" pursues an agenda that others would consider inauthentic or self-serving, and in this possibility we see the permanent fragility of political legitimacy. Also, as noted above, it may be that in the course of debate participants will challenge each other's traditionalist credentials, in an effort to delegitimize an opponent's claims. This may lead to what some call fundamentalism, a "purist" *surenchère* that could endanger democracy in a context where "purity" is always imagined. Modernity unavoidably lives within every member of aboriginal peoples in Canada, at the same time that many are formulating traditional(ist) identities for themselves.

"Purity" and tradition, in this sense, are never straightforward facts; they are rhetorical tropes, discursive strategies within which personal and collective projects are articulated. In other contexts, the critics of anti-democratic "purist" political discourses and practices have often mis-identified the faults of these movements. Thus, in the past fifteen years, a number of political movements across the globe have affirmed solidarities on the basis of tradition, whether ethno-national or religious, leading large numbers of Western intellectuals to warn of the dangers of "fundamentalism."[19] And fundamentalism, Anthony Giddens writes, is "always potentially dangerous. For it is a refusal of dialogue in circumstances where such dialogue is the only mode of mutual accommodation" (Giddens, 1994: 48).[20]

Refusal of dialogue, in the political realm, is indeed always dangerous for democracy. But it is not only "fundamentalism" that may be dangerous: no matter what political vocabulary one uses, no matter how ostensibly demo-

---

19 See for instance the otherwise very different Giddens (1994), Ignatieff (1993), and Mouffe (1994). This label of "fundamentalism" has been adapted for general use from the outlook of Christian sects that advocate a literal reading of the Bible. It has been widely noted, in particular with respect to political Islam, that the label is entirely inappropriate and not only because the term generally carries a pejorative connotation. By and large, "traditionalism" would seem to denote the same kind of political outlook as that of "fundamentalism," but with somewhat less of the stigma. This is certainly the case in Canadian discussions of aboriginal issues, where many members of aboriginal peoples would describe themselves as "traditionalist" while eschewing "fundamentalism."

20 Still, what *is* fundamentalism? Giddens writes that it is "tradition defended in the traditional way – but in response to novel circumstances of global communication." Clearly, this is not the case: fundamentalism does affirms the value of tradition, but certainly not "in the traditional way." From the audiotaped politics of the Ayatollah Khomeyni in the 1970s, to the university education in Arabic of young Algerians that energized that country's Islamist movement in the 1980s, emphatically non-traditional ways of being have been at the heart of "traditionalist" revivals. Indeed, this is what "isms" are all about. In this case, traditionalism is not tradition; it is the promotion of "tradition" in circumstances perceived as non-traditional.

cratic one's talk is, political practices are always underdetermined by the language that speaks them. This is not because language is not important, but rather because it is a context-sensitive practice. Think for instance of Stalin's Soviet constitution, which for decades was described (with increasing derision) as the most democratic in the world. This shows that the danger exists not only in aboriginal communities or Islamic societies, but also in the white stream.

More generally, every political discourse can provide the ground for purist *surenchère*, which is why defenders of democracy must always be vigilant, no matter what political discourse they inhabit. This is why many critiques of "fundamentalism" miss the mark, whether with regard to aboriginal peoples in Canada or, for instance, political Islam: they too readily locate dangers in the Other, allowing themselves to ignore the presence of the same demons in the interstices of whitestream democracy.

● ● ●

Given all this, let us come back to Joseph Peters, who was initiated into a spiritual tradition as (at least in part) a means of disciplining him. He might have been a Shaker Christian, or a convinced Catholic or Anglican for whom such rituals smack at least of paganism or even of the diabolical; or he might perhaps have been a hard-nosed materialist who had no truck for spirituality. This issue was not raised at trial,[21] and so we just do not know whether Peters held one of those beliefs.

What does that tell us about freedom of religion among self-governing aboriginal peoples? In a situation where at least part of the community sees no self-evident distinction between "the political" and "the religious," how are we to think of the co-existence in its midst of several spiritual outlooks?

Let us first note, once again, that we are not dealing with spiritual traditions that are entirely separate from each other: the absorption of Christianity in aboriginal communities has modified both native traditions and Christianity itself, through a merging of a variety of their tenets and practices. Thus, while it may be said that as abstract belief systems they are quite alien to each other, their actualization in individual men and women living in community has for quite a long time combined elements of both whether or not this was seen to be happening.

Two examples will illustrate the point. In the New France mission of Kanawake, the Iroquois woman Kateri Tekakwitha quickly acquired the reputation of a devout Catholic, with a particularly ardent spirituality; but the character of that spirituality drew heavily on aboriginal tradition (see

---

21 At least from what is given us by the text of the decision and the media reports.

Demos, 1994).[22] Among the Coast Salish people, we find a somewhat symmetrical situation: the practice of syewen is a "revival" that fed in part on the presence on the west coast of Shaker missions which practised a form of ecstatic Christianity (see Suttles, 1987).

The Coast Salish / Shaker connection also illustrates the tension bred in communities by the presence of individuals and groups that identify primarily with either the Shaker or the "traditional" pole of the relationship. Thus, soon after Joseph Peters launched his lawsuit, *The Regional News* interviewed Shaker members of the Salish communities near Islandtown, who were outraged at the coercive practices of the Longhouse (RN 4). The question remains: were something like Joseph Peters's "religious rights" violated? More widely, how are we to conceive of such an issue in the context of aboriginal communities?

It is important to keep in mind that spiritual belief and practice are (almost) always a matter of collective and institutional life: it is as a member of the Longhouse, or of the Anglican, Catholic, Shaker, or other church that a person will live her spirituality.[23] Given a decentralized system of aboriginal self-government, someone in Joseph Peters's situation (who wanted nothing to do with native tradition and culture) might have appealed to his own spiritual community for defence against another group seeking at once to discipline him and claim him as a member.

This of course requires that his own church (as the case may be) have "standing" within the Coast Salish community.[24] If so, he should be able to have his beliefs respected, and people seeking to discipline him would have to seek an alternative means of discipline. At worst, competition between spiritually-motivated groups would need to be somehow mediated in the context of the decentralized authority structure of self-government. It should not be forgotten, still, that the action against / on behalf of Joseph

---

22 The story of Kateri Tekakwitha was a mainstay of the "Histoire du Canada" classes in French Quebec at least until the mid-1960s, when I was in elementary school. She was a heroine of the Catholic enterprise in New France, and it goes without saying that our teachers did not talk about the aboriginal sources of her spirituality. As far as we were concerned, they did not exist. Some things seem to have changed little since the 1960s. One of the guided tours advertised in the programme of the 14th World Congress of Sociology, to be held in Montreal in 1998, is a visit to the Kanawake Mohawk Reserve; "the tour will include a visit to the church of Saint-François-Xavier's Mission where Kateri Tekakwitha's tombstone can be seen. A guide will tell the story of this Amerindian heroine and of the Mission" (*General Information and Registration Form*: 13).

23 One need not be a particularly active or even self-conscious member for this to be the case: allegiance to a tradition, rather than an institution will suffice.

24 Things are not that much more complicated in the case of those who would stand apart from spirituality altogether: in any given community such people also form a constituency, which may be able to obtain standing in a manner similar to that of a church such that their a-spirituality would be respected.

Peters was taken at the behest of his wife, and in a manner that she thought acceptable.

If, on the other hand, the reluctant initiate's beliefs are not recognized as legitimate (as a variety of sects and cults are not deemed legitimate in whitestream societies), other issues arise. It could be that the community needs to re-evaluate the boundaries of what it considers acceptable and perhaps find that things are fine as they are. In any case, we have a conflict here that needs to be adjudicated. The question, as ever, is by whom: a whitestream court applying whitestream laws, or self-governing aboriginal peoples?

Aboriginal peoples in Canada and elsewhere have for a long time been living with a plurality of spiritual outlooks. In such communities, where political legitimacy is drawn from a variety of sources, one of which is the spiritual realm, public authority is necessarily decentralized. They may well be able, as a result, to respect spiritual pluralism at least as adequately as whitestream societies have been doing recently. As for whitestream societies' past, it would be ill-advised for anyone to seek a good example there.

● ● ●

Spirituality, in this chapter, has been treated in the context of its place in society and politics and in terms of the accommodation of pluralism. Framed in this way, it cannot be detached from sociostructural processes and issues of social control and moral regulation (see Bastide, 1972, 1975; and de Certeau, 1987). And, as with any sociological analysis, (issues of) freedom should be envisaged as situated, for social rules are always at once constricting and enabling (Giddens, 1976). Thus, one of the striking things about the usual process of initiation into syewen is that one of its roles is to tame a trance-like "sickness" that develops in certain individuals (Suttles, 1987). From the time of the initiation and for several years afterwards, such individuals learn to channel their "sickness" in ways that are acceptable to the community, under the direction and guidance of accredited members of the community. Roger Bastide has described a similar process of "socializing," "moulding" trance in Africa and Brazil (Bastide, 1972).[25]

In such terms of sociological analysis, spirituality is almost bound to be seen as a means to an end. But this is to deny it the analytical autonomy that it ought to claim. There is, in other words, the question of spirituality for itself, rather than in the context of social control. That is the burden of the next chapter.

---

25 Bastide draws a terminological distinction that need not overly detain us between trance, which is raw, individual and "savage," and possession, which is "trance captured through the collective representations of a group, and as such a 'cultural' phenomenon" (1972: 74; my translation).

Chapter 7
Limit-experience

←───→

There is no Buddha outside one's mind.[1]

Being uniquely of this continent, the language of aboriginal spirituality would seem like the most appropriate way for me to approach issues of the limit-experience,[2] more so than, say, an appeal to Zen Buddhism. This is surely the case, and especially since I got to this point through a consideration of Joseph Peters's syewen initiation. But, as the discussion in Chapter 2 on my relationship to aboriginal peoples and cultures has argued, the most direct approach in this case is not actually appropriate. I wrote that I did not want to describe syewen in any more detail than was necessary, because many members of First Nations are not only reluctant to discuss such spiritual practices, but are very unhappy with descriptions of their cultures by outsiders who, it seems, generally misunderstand what they are seeing and what they are told.

I am certainly not immune to misunderstanding, and it is only prudent to respect the cautions against inadvertently demeaning accounts.[3] One last example of the difficulty will illustrate the point. The court and newspaper descriptions of Joseph Peters's initiation include the fact that, in the process of being initiated, he was supposed to sing a song expressing his personal relationship with his guardian spirit. What kind of song are we talking about? Thus far, I have avoided discussing this, and have left standing the very limited (and flat) description, despite the possibly trivial images that it may evoke. Such an initiatory song is anything but trivial, however, as Cree Elder Joseph Couture indicates when quoting a "frequent saying" of many elders: "Everybody has a song to sing which is no song at all: it is a process

---

1 John C.H. Wu (1996: 71), paraphrasing the classical master Ma-tsu Tao-i (709-788), who was following the insights of Hui-neng, Zen's Sixth Patriarch.

2 For the discussion of what "the limit-experience" is, see the Introduction and Chapter 1.

3 Some features of syewen establishing it as a limit-experience and a form of mysticism are described in the Introduction and in Chapters 3, 4, and 6.

of singing, and when you sing, you are where you are" (Couture, 1991: 61). There is something quite mysterious going on here, that is closely related to Zen formulations. In the elders' saying, and presumably in the initiation itself, the word song functions in a deeply altered way. In a text such as Judge Hood's decision in *Peters v. Campbell*, this mystery is entirely missing from the ordinary language sentence "the initiate sings a song."

The issue, moreover, is not only one of a correct apprehension of something like syewen. It is one of ethical and political respect for the protection members of First Nations want to afford their spiritual practices. One consequence of this reserve is that, in this chapter on spirituality and limit-experience, I will say very little about syewen in general or the initiation of Joseph Peters in particular. I will, rather, look at the spiritual indigence of modernity that is brought into sharp relief by the *Peters v. Campbell* affair. In this perspective, specifically Canadian issues will not be prominent, but the general issues of modernity that will be raised do have their Canadian iteration.

This last chapter thus brings us to the most radical lesson that aboriginality has in store for modernity. As we shall see below, modernity has banned limit-experience as a transgressive form of practice, as belonging to the outside of its cultural framework. This banishment, highly specific to modernity, marks it as a remarkably poor grand narrative on the spiritual world-map. As Joseph Couture writes of "Native mindfullness" or "the medicine ways," while aboriginal spirituality has a unique relationship to this continent, it is an approach in which "non-dualistic knowing balances all relationships, individual and 'communitarian'" (Couture, 1991: 53-5). As such, it shares much with other spiritual outlooks commonly described as mystically oriented.

Contrary to the self-satisfied notions of those who raise the separation of church and state (from its history of ameliorating problems particular to European history) to the status of a universal principle, I will argue that modernity has solved nothing in the relationship between spirituality and public life. If anything, when compared with a wide range of practices – of which syewen is one of the most immediately present to (and hidden from) us – modernity's outlook on spirituality subtracts from the beauty of which humanity is capable. In this connection, I will highlight intercultural parallels, or affinities, in a variety of forms of human practice that can be described as limit-experience.

This chapter is, I am afraid, the book's most theoretical – if that is the proper word to indicate the generality of its propositions and its interpellation of philosophers. This also makes it the most difficult. A consolation may be that, at this point, we are almost home.

● ● ●

The last time the kind of spirituality characteristic of the limit-experience had any kind of mainstream vocation in the West was with the radical branch of the seventeenth century Puritan revolution in England.[4] The Levellers, Ranters, and other Antinomians rejected the Moral Law (that is, the Ten Commandments) in favour of "free grace" and the Everlasting Gospel. This was / is a form of mysticism in which the believer would develop a direct relationship with Christ, leading to spiritual enlightenment[5] unmediated by the the strictures of churches and clergies, or indeed by the Ten Commandments themselves. This "doctrine of justification by faith … displaced the authority of institutions and of received worldly wisdom with that of the individual's inner light … and allowed the individual a stubborn scepticism in the face of the established culture, a fortitude in the face of its seductions or persecutions" (Thompson, 1993: 5). But in the political and religious struggles of their time, these radicals lost to more sober, polite and bourgeois outlooks (see Hill, 1972).

On the European continent, the sixteenth and seventeenth centuries were also the scene of waves of mysticism, developing along a dynamic different from that in England and Scotland. In Spain, France and Germany, mysticism was expressed not only in the new literary genre which Michel de Certeau (1987) has called the "mystic fable," but also in spiritual movements such as Jansenism that were deeply involved in those two centuries' wars of religion.[6] These forms of spirituality, de Certeau writes, burned out as the *siècle des Lumières* was beginning.

Note the centrality of the seventeenth century moment in the genesis of modernity. These religious struggles brought about not only the defeat of mystically oriented forms of Christianity, but also the rise of the doctrine of the separation of church and state. We have seen that this doctrine functions as ideology without being fully anchored in institutions and/or political practice in such countries as Canada, the United States, and the United

---

4   Not that the radicals were the mainstream. While their exact placement in the political-religious constellation of their time is the subject of heated controversy, it seems clear that they were speaking the same cultural language as other, less exalted groups; they were, however, taking that language to the interpretative limit of what it would tolerate. We will see below that current descendants of the most radical Puritans speak an entirely different language from that of the modern polity. On the very contested history of the Puritans, see William Lamont's (1996) highly useful review of the debates and the evidence.

5   The so-called "Age of Reason", the eighteenth century, is of course refered to as "the Enlightenment." I will distinguish this, with a capital "e," from the mystical enlightenment found in Zen, aboriginal spirituality, and the Dissenting English sects.

6   These movements had their impact in New France, the development of which had its mystically oriented component. Montreal, in particular, was founded by "a group of religious mystics in France who were moved by visions to build a missionary city in the wilderness…" (Christopher Moore in Brown [ed.], 1987: 116). Marie de l'Incarnation, one of New France's "founding mothers," was also a mystic (see Mettayer, 1988).

Kingdom. Similarly, the defeat of the radical Puritans, the last community of mystically oriented modern Christians, does not mean that they disappeared altogether: they (and their outlook) have been pushed to the fringes of modern culture, where they survive, often almost invisibly, as increasingly eccentric remnants.

At the end of the eighteenth century, "polite and rational religious culture" was victorious throughout Europe, but retained uneasy memories of the previous century's religious wars on the continent and of the religious "enthusiasm" of England's Civil War. This is when a last wave of mystical spirituality hit the UK and North America. Faced with a surge of mysticism which it still feared, "polite" culture responded by looking down upon contemporary enthusiasts "(a)nd the derisory judgement which the learned and the accomplished then made upon these enthusiasts still imposes itself upon us today. We see them only as eccentrics or as survivors ... they are quaint historical fossils" (Thompson, 1993: 107-8). The radical / mystic protestant sects were thus pushed ever further into anti-Enlightenment and irrationalism (Thompson, 1993: 86).

In North America, the second half of the eighteenth century also saw the last widespread movement affirming a radical and mystical protestantism, in the context and aftermath of the American revolution. Thus, Nova Scotia, as well as the New England colonies, went through a "Great Awakening" with leaders such as the reverend Henry Alline, who experienced "the intense ecstasy of spiritual rapture" and expected his followers to do so along with him (Rawlyk, 1984: 5). The key, once again, was "a personal relationship with Christ," allowing Alline to preach Free Grace and taking some of his immediate spiritual descendants to the "antinomian breaking point" (Rawlyk, 1984: 9, 14, 81).

As the nineteenth century began, the process of disciplining these groups into what became the Baptist Church was well under way (Rawlyk, 1984). In the United States, however, radical protestantism found yet more means of expression with the founding of such churches as the Seventh Day Adventist, the Mormons, and the Shakers (Lamont, 1996). The latter, as we have seen, found their way to the Pacific and played a role in the twentieth-century spirituality of West-coast aboriginal peoples. Although these churches held (and hold) considerable popular appeal, they have become increasingly marginal to the culture of modernity.

The antinomian stance had become so foreign to the victorious modern outlook that, by the middle of the nineteenth century, the spirituality and aesthetic of an artist and poet such as William Blake (who died in 1827) had become largely indecipherable (see Thompson, 1993). Blake is even more a stranger to us, at the end of the twentieth century. This cultural estrangement shows how profound the transformations of the last 150 years have been in the West. In its aggressive secularism[7] and, especially, its anti-mysticism, the world in which we live is about as remote from a relatively recent European past as it is from aboriginal spirituality or Zen. It is hard to grasp, for example, the trust that such men as Isaac Newton, Francis Bacon, John Locke, and Oliver Cromwell put in various forms of magic, alchemy, and astrology (see Hill, 1972). More to the point of this study, our knowledge-obsessed culture is bound to find alien and offensive the antinomians' distrust of knowledge, who thought that Reason is the work of Satan (Thompson, 1993: 94-6). Such a distrusts finds a significant parallel in Zen's call to reach beyond the mind. In "native knowing" as well, Enlightenment-style reason takes a backseat: "... the traditional 'world' of indigenous knowledge is a sense-world which is in truth spiritual" (Couture, 1991: 66).

● ● ●

The antinomian stance was radically individualist in its outlook on spiritual enlightenment. But this does not mean that it was developed by socially isolated individuals. Quite the contrary. The antinomian approach developed in the context of small communities of fierce believers, gathered around a charismatic leader. In this respect, the rise of antinomian movements can be connected to specific social coordinates, relating both to the individuals who are likely to be attracted to radical spiritual communities and to the historical circumstances that spawn such communities. In this sense, it is easy for sociological reason to "disenchant" radical spiritual practices by showing that social circumstances gave them birth.[8] It is basic sociological reasoning, and it goes like this: these people may think that they have a privileged relationship with God, but the reason why these particular individuals think these particular thoughts is that they belong to social groups that are insecure for economic, cultural, or some other reasons. As an expression of a rationalist worldview, such reasoning is unassailable. But another spin can be put on the relationship: in certain circumstances, the inadequacies of social life can be made plain to certain categories of people who will draw their own conclusions in terms allowed by their cultural context.

Some readers of the above outline of radical sects may be put in mind of David Koresh, his "Branch Davidian" sect, and their fiery end in Waco, Texas in 1993. While other readers may find it outrageous, this is a true par-

---

7   While officially secular*ist*, the modern world is anything but secular*ized*. The same sort of distinction applies to words such as modern and postmodern on the one hand, and modern*ist* and postmodern*ist* on the other.

8   See for instance de Certeau (1987) and Kent (1987).

allel to the history of past Puritan communities, not in particular actions, but in the stance adopted by such sects against established cultural and religious forms, in some of its theological positions, and in its aggressive mysticism. Indeed, in *Puritanism and Historical Controversy*, William Lamont writes that Koresh's "sect did not come from nowhere. The "Branch Davidian"move-ment was an off-shoot of the Seventh Day Adventists," who were themselves descendants of other Puritans (Lamont, 1996: 129). "It is good historical sense then to see Koresh, not simply in pathological terms (as, fatally, the Texan authorities[9] did), but in eschatological terms, as belonging to a long tradition of American puritan millenialism" (Lamont, 1996: 129-130).

That mystical spirituality would make rare public appearances in so prob-lematic a form (and with such tragic consequences)[10] speaks to the thor-oughness with which it has been pushed out of modernity's mainstream. Not that intense and, indeed, mystical spirituality is generally absent from societies where the modern grand narrative is dominant. Mystical spiritual-ity is in fact thriving at the margin of the modern cultural project, notwith-standing the evolutionist tradition in social sciences that has claimed that the modern world is increasingly secular. Such notions are what we find in the otherwise up-to-the-minute work of Bryan Turner: "... at the level of everyday life, the relativization of belief via commodities, travel, tourism and the impact of global TV shakes the bases of faith in the general popula-tion" (Turner, 1994: 17).[11]

This view is consistent with old theories which held that modernization was supposed to put an end to religious belief. But it is just not accurate. More than twenty years ago, Roger Bastide argued that the crisis of main-line religion not only in the West but also in Islam stemmed from the gap between institutional imperatives of the established Churches and the needs of "personal religious experience" (Bastide, 1975: 214).[12] Deriding the soci-ological conventional wisdom of secularization, Bastide went on to ask: "are

---

9   American federal authorities were in fact in charge of the law enforcement operation in Waco. The FBI became involved late in the stand-off. The Bureau of Alcohol, Tobacco and Firearms (known as ATF) had set the siege and assaulted the Branch Davidians' compound, which Koresh and his followers were calling Mount Carmel, after the mountain in Palestine where, accord-ing to the Bible, Elijah defeated the prophets of Baal (I Kings 17, II Kings 2); tradition also makes that mountain the origin of the Carmelite order, of which the mystics John of the Cross and Teresa of Avila were members.

10 In Canada, France, and Switzerland, the no less tragic end of the Cult of the Solar Temple tells a similar story without, admittedly, the specific theological precedent of the Puritans.

11 Rawlyk's (1996) extensive survey of the Canadian population's religious beliefs in the 1990s provides a flat rebuttal to this notion of shaken bases of faith. More on this below.

12 One might think that the rise of a radicalized political Islam from the late 1970s in Iran to today in such places as Algeria and Egypt is, among other things, an outcome of this crisis.

we not witnessing today a new passionate search for the sacred among the young(?)"[13]

From the rise of political Islam (on which Turner himself writes), to the political prominence of the "Christian right" in the US Republican Party, the popularity of New Age beliefs and Eastern philosophies,[14] and the proliferation of cults, sects, and psychic healing, it should be clear that "the general population" in any number of Western (and other) countries has not turned away from religious belief in all its variety, including and in particular from intense and highly personalized spiritual encounters. On the contrary, while many mainstream, "polite and rational" churches have been declining, creeds that focus on individualized and intense spiritual experience have been growing at remarkable rates. Thus, Harvey Cox notes that Pentecostalism, "by far the fastest-growing wing of Christianity today," owes its "astonishing global growth ... to its emphasis on experience rather than doctrine and to its capacity to absorb such local spiritual practices as ancestor veneration in Africa, folk healing in South America, and shamanic trance in Korea" (Cox, 1995: 62, 61).

But "absorb" may be the wrong word for Cox to use, and it might be better to talk of syncretism, or indeed interculturalism. The point is that (for instance) Pentecostalism's emphasis on the direct (if always culturally mediated) spiritual experience of individuals rather than on doctrine allows for the development of much common / middle ground among people living in different cultural languages. In more doctrine-oriented creeds, one might say that the grand narrative gets in the way of communication.

The "Christian right" in the United States is particularly important here, both in terms of sociopolitical trends and forms of spirituality. This brand of Christianity is often pooled under the general label of "Evangelical," but Cox finds this rather too vague. He identifies five main strands within the Christian right: the Born-again, who claim "a personal experience with Christ," including as much as 39% of the US population; the Evangelicals, who claim not only that same experience, but also the obligation to share it with others, and a strong reliance on Scripture; the Fundamentalists, who add to this a literal reading of the Bible; the Pentecostals, for whom ecstatic experience is primary and theology secondary, resulting in a "sometimes chaotic and unpredictable spirituality"; and the Charismatics, who may remain members of mainline churches, but "practise a Pentecostal form of worship" (Cox, 1995: 62). Sara Diamond reports that, in the 1994 US mid-

---

13 Lest one thinks that the "secularization" conventional wisdom has been superseded since Bastide's 1973 lecture, see Ammerman (1994), cited in Rawlyk (1996: 224-225).

14 Thus, John C.H. Wu, writing in 1967 of the surging popularity of Zen and other Eastern philosophies, noted that "the young generation in the West ... feels ill at ease with the neatly defined concepts and dogmas of their traditional religion" (Wu, 1996: 30).

term elections, "(n)ationwide exit polls indicated that evangelical Christians comprised about 30 percent of those who voted"; and that "the Christian right won victories for 60 percent of the candidates the movement backed" (Diamond, 1995: 2). The outlook of such conservative Christians may be marginal to our dominant cultural model, modernity; but no matter how one counts, these people have been numerous and influential enough to move politics in North America significantly to the right.

G.W. Rawlyk, the Canadian student of evangelicalism, has written that he was "repelled" by the evangelical-fundamentalist movement in the Southern United States when he travelled there in 1994. This religious environment "discouraged, depressed, and profoundly alienated" him, and he found this form of Christianity "frightening and disconcerting" (Rawlyk, 1996: 3, 4). He realized how different Canadian evangelicals are from their American cousins. This does not mean, as his book *Is Jesus Your Personal Saviour?* shows, that Canadian evangelicals are meek mainline Church followers: in wide-ranging opinion surveys, Rawlyk found that there is (and has been) "a huge gap between élite and popular Christianity in Canada" (Rawlyk, 1996: 224). While English Canada's "liberal Protestant hegemony" has been collapsing along with Quebec's Catholic Church, the number of committed evangelicals and charismatics[15] has been growing rapidly. Thus, it is significant that a 1993 survey found that 62% of Canadians "strongly or moderately agree that they have actually experienced God's presence in their lives" (Rawlyk, 1996: 59).

To feel God's presence is a notable marker of conservative Christianity, and more specifically of a form of spirituality that is open to ecstatic experience. But it overshoots the mark of identification with evangelicalism. Rawlyk found that approximately 15% of Canadians in the first half of the 1990s claimed to be evangelical Christians. And while Rawlyk pays little attention to politics, it is clear that this group belongs among the most conservative of Canadians.

● ● ●

As mentioned earlier, some may be outraged by the inclusion in the same discussion of David Koresh with eighteenth century sects and William Blake, and more widely with native spirituality and Zen. Even considering native spirituality side by side with the "Christian right" may seem awful. It

---

15 While "evangelicals" have risen from within the Protestant Churches, the charismatic movement spans the Protestant-Catholic divide, in what Rawlyk calls "a revolutionary development" (Rawlyk, 1996: 81). He characterizes the charismatic Christian as "having a profound religious experience involving the Holy Spirit following conversion," with conversion understood as being born again (Rawlyk, 1996: 87). This results in Rawlyk including Roman Catholics among evangelicals to the tune of one-third of the Canadian total (Rawlyk, 1996: 118).

provides a nice target for critics of postmodern and other relativist perspectives, who like to berate them for bowing to every local practice,[16] not to mention the unpleasantness of guilt by association to disreputable people and outlooks. But the point is to make distinctions *between* these practices cast out by modernity, not to lump them all together.

There is more than specifically religious belief, discourse or language involved here, in that "the speaking of language is part of an activity, or of a form of life." (Wittgenstein, 1968: §23; emphasis in the original). In a "form of life," various kinds of beliefs and practices are integrated and articulated to each other, not necessarily without tensions. Such articulations are not specifically dictated by logic, but rather by the circumstances in which the form of life develops. Thus, American "conservative Christians," who are on the margins of modernity in terms of their spirituality and approach to the political, also have specific socio-political and geographic coordinates: they tend to live in the South, and to be among the most conservative people in the United States. While rather more moderate, Canadian evangelicals also share in that conservatism. As G.A. Rawlyk has written of their outlook: "... leaders, and now a growing number of followers [of contemporary North American evangelicalism] have been enamoured with consumerism and a crude form of capitalism" (Rawlyk, 1996: 223).

Specifically, the conservative Christians' project of injecting their religious vision into the structure and practice of government so as to strictly discipline the people, challenges the very core of secularist modernity's politics.[17] This is best seen in their most radical branch, "dominion theology," which according to Cox (1995) may inform the theology and politics of Pat Robertson, the leader of the Christian Coalition, the movement at the core of the number one constituency in the Republican Party (Diamond, 1995).[18] Dominion theology claims that, because of Adam and Eve's God-given mandate to "have dominion ... over every living thing that moveth upon the earth" (Genesis, 1:28), believers have the right and duty to rule the earth. They are "entitled to 'dominion' over all the world's major institutions. They should rule the earth until Christ comes again, no matter what the

---

16 I return to this issue in the Conclusion, to show that this criticism is indefensible, both theoretically and practically.

17 In this disciplining project, the Christian right shares a number of important goals with the promoters of neo-liberal economics, the two outlooks forming together what is typically known as the "new right." On the new right's project of moral regulation in the Canadian context, see Denis (1995). But the American Christian right's constitutive need to break the secularism of government has so far placed a ceiling on its political reach, even as it has become the strongest single component of the Republican Party. On the American right and the tensions between its components, see Diamond (1995).

18 On Pat Robertson, the Christian Coalition and the Republican Party, see also Lind (1995) and J. Taylor (1994).

duration of their interim reign" (Cox, 1995: 66; see also Diamond, 1995: 246-249). Diamond writes that soft forms of dominion theology – the general ideas that "America was ordained as a Christian nation and that Christians, exclusively, were to rule and reign" – have "a wide following" (Diamond, 1995: 248).

In North America, the forms of life of people who speak the spiritual languages of Eastern philosophies or aboriginal spirituality are considerably different. And, as liberation theology[19] shows, there is no necessary connection between strong Christian beliefs and right-wing politics. By the same token, while there are significant historical and theoretical linkages between today's "conservative Christians" and seventeenth and eighteenth century Puritans, their respective situations set them at sharply different points on the political spectrum. This, indeed, is the political dimension of a disjunction much debated in sociology since at least Max Weber's The *Protestant Ethic and the Spirit of Capitalism.* In the early days of capitalism, radical Protestantism could anchor forms of life favouring increased commercial activity and parliamentarism against landed wealth and absolute monarchy,[20] placing this religious stance, in our terms, on the left of the political spectrum. Later capitalist development freed itself altogether from the ethic of Protestant asceticism, and as the mainline churches became increasingly rational and polite, radical Protestants moved to the margins, and eventually to the far right.

It is interesting, however, that in all the Weberian emphasis on Protestant asceticism as a rationalizing force and creator of the modern sense of inner self (see Sayer, 1991), there is something missing: the intense, exalted, sometimes mystical spiritual experience which was the goal of this asceticism and could only come about in an "inner self." It seems that this spiritual exaltation of the Puritans is largely invisible to secularized twentieth century students of the "spirit of capitalism;" it is not *"dans le vrai"*, as Foucault (1971) wrote. It is so foreign to us that we look right through it as if it were not there. Analysis of contemporary culture in North America is afflicted with the same blind spot: the large-scale presence of mystically oriented Christianity is largely ignored when portraying our surroundings, except when some remarkable event (e.g. the Waco disaster) happens, or when an important figure admits to such beliefs (e.g. President Reagan's admission that he believed in the Rapture).[21]

---

19 At the centre of liberation theology is a "preferential option for the poor"; it "aims to work for institutions that are responsive to the poor and disinherited of any society" (Cox, 1995: 69).

20 I am not claiming that there was a necessary connection in the English Revolution between radical Protestantism and Parliament; debate among specialists remains rife on this issue (see Lamont, 1996). I am merely saying that there were radical Protestants who articulated their faith in ways supportive of Parliament against the Crown.

21 In Evangelical belief, Rapture is the moment when the righteous are physically lifted to heaven while still living, just as the Apocalypse engulfs the rest of us.

• • •

So modernity has not eliminated mystically oriented forms of spirituality. What modernity has accomplished, however, is not only the ideological separation of church and state, but also the complete delegitimation of mystical spirituality. Clearly, this separation / delegitimation has a limited purchase among "the general population" of a number of countries, including Canada. More critically, in the United States, the Christian right wields huge political influence at the same time that the lack of legitimacy of its outlook in the dominant grand narrative of modernity has contributed in pushing evangelicalism to rightist extremes that might otherwise have been avoided. In any case, the tension bred by this mixture of influence and illegitimacy cannot but be dangerous.

Secularized intellectuals who are even willing to face this cultural divide, are likely to look at it and bemoan the backwardness of the masses. At worst, this amounts to adapting to our own difficulties the old Soviet-bloc joke: the alienation between the people and the Party is so great that the Party is thinking of electing a new people. At best, we (the intellectuals) will say that we have not been doing our job of educating the public; we may also blame the brutalizing cultural manifestations of capitalism, through commodified pop culture and the mass media. At least some of this diagnosis has value: intellectuals are not communicating very effectively outside academia,[22] and a good part of capital-driven pop culture is indeed brutalizing. But something else ought to be consided as well. We ought to listen to what is being said so loudly, and take it seriously: modernity's marginalizing of spirituality is a severely debilitating flaw.

It is in this context of delegitimized mystical spirituality that, in serious philosophical discourse, the limit-experience only finds expression as something anti-social, transgressive, "the outside." Western philosophy since Nietzsche, from Heidegger to Georges Bataille and Michel Foucault, has developed a whole branch that affirms this transgression, seeking to break through modern understandings. In so doing, it feeds on a long tradition in the West of engagement with *fecund transgression*, such as may emerge for instance from the exalted believer's withdrawal to the desert, the forest, or the mountain in medieval Europe. Some of these men and women have, after the fact, been hailed as saints and visionaries; but as they were withdrawing, chances are that they were thought crazy or dangerous in their

---

22 And this is not merely an issue of the critical intellectuals being poor communicators. The message that would be communicated is often anti-capitalist, anti-consumerist, and so on. It is to be expected that commercial publishers, television networks, and their like would not be overly excited by this and the same goes for potential audiences who tend to be fully involved in consumerism and pop culture. The vocation of critical intellectuals is, to a significant extent then, to speak without being heard. Why even speak? Because certain things must be said.

rejection of society and courting of the dangers of the wild. Many such hermits and mystics surely disappeared without a trace, but a few became cultural heroes – "saints" – and their craziness was validated as fecund transgression (see Lemieux, 1988B).

Foucault writes that "(i)nterrogating a culture on its limit-experiences,[23] is to question it at the far reaches of history, on a tear that is something like the very birth of its history" (Foucault, 1994D: 161). Thus, we may learn much about ourselves by looking at our taboos, and at how they came into being in relation to those other things that are non-taboo. It is in this perspective of putting taboos in question that Bataille is keen to detach eroticism, which he understands as "assenting to life up to the point of death" (Bataille, 1986: 11), from anything having to do with morality (see Bataille, 1989). This opens the door wide to his inquiry into eroticism from its physical to its religious dimensions, that embraces the necessary ritual transgression of taboos, and the links between pain and pleasure, sensuality and death – and ecstasy.

Foucault's contrasting of Western modernity's *scientia sexualis* to the *ars erotica* of other civilizations (China, India, Japan, Rome) explores some of the same terrain (Foucault, 1976). Bataille's attempt to face the tear in Western culture regarding eroticism is nicely hinted at by this dichotomy of Foucault's. If the West deals with sex in terms of science and morality, it becomes clear what Bataille is doing with his claim to work "in contradiction to the scientific method" (Bataille, 1986: 7) and his assertion of "the absurdity of any connection between eroticism and morality" (Bataille, 1989: 19): situating his work at the structural birth of Western history, he is reclaiming something of its outside.

It is Foucault's "history of madness in the classical age" (Foucault, 1972)[24] that offers his most explicit philosophical work on the limit-experience: "in the constitution of madness as mental illness, at the end of the xvIIIth century," Foucault studies the establishment of limits through which Western reason "rejects something that will be its Outside" (Foucault, 1994D: 160-1). Thus, madness will be the "indecipherable delirium," indeed the silence, that is the other side of reason's ability to make sense. This is why "reason cannot exist, in our culture, without madness" (Foucault, 1994D: 162-3).

---

23 In this formulation, the limit-experience is culture-specific: something like saying, to each culture its taboos. I have been designating limit-experience in its structural dimension, relating to the nature of the relationship between language and world.

24 That book was originally Foucault's main doctoral thesis defended in 1960 and published in 1961 under the title *Folie et déraison: Histoire de la folie à l'âge classique*. A new edition was published in 1972, which dropped the first half of the title, the preface and appendices, and added a new preface. The widely available English translation *Madness and Civilization*, contains less than half the text found in the French editions. The 1961 preface, a remarkable text, has been reproduced as Foucault (1994D).

Needless to say, another branch of Western philosophy has been resisting this enterprise of questioning modernity by affirming the transgressions that distinguish it from its outside. This other branch points to moral and political dangers presumably inherent to the Nietzschean leanings at the source of a philosophical interest in transgression. In this connection, the scandal of Heidegger's momentary association with National Socialism, not to mention Nietzsche's posthumous (and outrageously fraudulent) appropriation by the Nazis, are particularly notorious. They function as archetypes of the sins to which transgressive philosophy leads. Heidegger's thought, for instance, has been characterized as "ethically indifferent" to the point of "consenting to the horror" of the Holocaust (Levinas, 1989: 487).

In striving to re-establish contact with Being – a concept "that can be compared with ... the 'all-in-one' of Zen" (Donoghue, 1996: 37) – of which modernity has been estranged, Heidegger echoes and enacts Nietzsche's call to go beyond morality.[25] In this sense, the critique of ethical indifference stands, but at the price of dragging Heidegger's project back onto a philosophical plane which he rejects. And this is the problem with critiques that derive theoretically necessary conclusions about the politics of such philosophers as Nietzsche, Heidegger, and Foucault, from philosophies in which the political is a secondary and contingent concern.[26] Just as it is a hopeless task to try to place Nietzsche on a left-right political spectrum, it is inappropriate (and indeed meaningless) to tax Heidegger of ethical indifference and Foucault of "conservatism."[27]

We have in Heidegger's longing for Being (and his finding it in the exceptionality of Hölderlin's poetry), Western philosophy's and modernity's inability to think of the limit-experience as anything other than the exception, the a- or anti-social. But limit-experience need not be transgressive of social rules. Bastide has written, for instance, that trance "constitutes for a very great number of religions, a normal phenomenon, culturally instituted and directed – what am I saying, normal? compulsory and sanctioned" (Bastide, 1975: 216; my translation).

---

25 See for instance *Beyond Good and Evil*, § 33 (in my French edition: Nietzsche, 1993B).

26 My claim here is that Foucault's work should not be interpreted as involving a political philosophy. This goes against the bulk of Foucault scholarship, which is much concerned with the politics of Foucault's work (see for instance Best, 1995; and Dumm, 1996). Unfortunately, I cannot argue this case here, beyond noting this: I understand Foucault's attitude to the political as strategic, based on a theoretically coherent *refusal* of modernity's ontology of politics; that is to say, the sense that human history is on a path of progress that is increasingly politically directed. This is one way in which Foucault fundamentally parts company with Jürgen Habermas (see note 27 below).

27 In current philosophy, the most substantial and hyped on-going controversy in these matters is the so-called Foucault-Habermas debate – Habermas having argued that Foucault was a "young conservative". See Best (1995) and, for a Habermas-friendly take, Fraser (1989).

In Eastern philosophy, and in aboriginal spirituality, the limit-experience is something fully integrated in social life, emerging from routinized social interaction, not weird or deviant, but normal, necessary, and even honoured. George Woodcock, writing of the "spirit quest" among the Coast Salish people before European contact, notes that this was a practice in which most adults of both sexes engaged – a markedly democratic pattern perhaps stemming from that society's low level of social inequality (Woodcock, 1990). Pentecostal Christians in the United States, in whose prayer meetings one may become suddenly entranced and start "speaking in tongues," also form a community in which the limit-experience is socially integrated.

• • •

The contemporary spiritual challenge to modernity, then, comes from various points on the political spectrum: right, left, and indeed from somewhere perpendicular to that axis. And it is most radical, in fact, in its perpendicularity to politics. This challenge is postmodern in a weak sense through its critique of the political grand narrative of secularism, which is constitutive of modernity, a political narrative which authors such as Jürgen Habermas are insistent on defending. Not only do large portions of populations not subscribe to this ideology, but they seek forms of spirituality spurned by modernity and its polite churches, in which limit-experience is relegated to the domain of transgression. Considered in this sociological way, however, there is no getting out of power relations. Even highly individual experience is situated in networks of social relations and the exercise of institutional and/or interpersonal power. Thus, the initiation of Joseph Peters involved the limit-experience as a component of social control.

The strong postmodern challenge, in the face of this context, is a consideration of limit-experience for its own, spiritual, sake – at the limit, on the razor's edge[28] of society's power relations. This is the main burden of how I want to conclude this chapter. Readers steeped in postmodern theory may think this claim paradoxical, if not perverse, for at least two reasons. First, some of postmodernism's best theoretical anchors are the Nietzchean / Foucauldian "death of God / Man"[29] claims, which may seem ill-suited to

---

28 Once again, I am misusing for my own purposes a phrase otherwise known. *The Razor's Edge* (New York: P.F. Collier, 1944) is W. Somerset Maugham's novel of one man's spiritual search, one of those rare "persons who do things simply for the love of God whom they don't believe in" (202). Maugham borrowed his title from a saying in the Katha-Upanishad, which he quotes on the novel's title page: "The sharp edge of a razor is difficult to pass over; thus the wise say the path to Salvation is hard." There is, I would think, a rich family resemblance between the saying's point and the use to which I am putting the phrase.

29 On the notorious claim that man is dead: what does Foucault mean in *The Order of Things* (*Les mots et les choses*) when he says that "before the end of the 18th century, *man* did not exist," and he will soon disappear? Gutting explains that: "The term (man) does not refer to human beings

backing an autonomous-spirituality argument. The second reason can be formulated as a question: is it defensible to offer this argument if we post-modernists are to be seriously sceptical toward grand narratives?

It is important, first, to avoid importing vaguely Marxian understandings in our reading of Nietzsche and Foucault's pronouncements on God and Man. Marx, learning from Feuerbach, argued that religious belief was a false consciousness that served to obscure social injustice. In *The Gay Science*,[30] Nietzsche made fun of such notions, suggesting that they were nothing more than intellectual vulgarity. While it is always difficult (if not impossi-ble) to pin down a core message in Nietzsche's writing, it is clear that he did not agree with this materialist claim that "Man created God." But that does not tell us what (if anything specific) he did mean when writing "God is dead."

The theoretical logic of Foucault's "death of Man" is plainer to see. "Man" is a character, a representational figure, constructed at the end of the eighteenth and the beginning of the nineteenth centuries. This figure is in the process of being disarticulated by "contemporary analytical reason" as pioneered by Bertrand Russell and later by structural linguistics and anthro-pology (Foucault, 1994C).[31] "Man", then, is a component of a discourse, quite recent and perhaps on the way to be replaced by other figures in an always transforming discursive landscape.

The outcome of Foucault's discourse-theoretical move is the advent of the decentred subject – in analytical terms, the displacement of the subject from the primary position to a secondary, derived, one. At the same time, language / discourse acquires a primacy that reaches far beyond issues of research methods.[32] In the moment of this privileging, discourse theory encounters both the *infinity* of discourse and its *limit*. What is meant by this? Before going to a consideration, in turn, of infinity and the limit, let us look at an example: the pronoun "I" and its relationship to me. In an ordinary situation, if you want to tell someone that you are leaving the house, you may say "I am going out." You do not need to consider the fact that "I" is

---

as a biological species nor even to their psychological and social reality except insofar as it involves representation." The question is whether "the human power of representation is or is not an object of knowledge for that area"; if it is not, *man* does not exist (Gutting, 1989: 198-9). See also "L'homme est-il mort?" (Foucault, 1994C), an interview Michel Foucault gave after the publication of *Les mots et les choses* in 1966.

30 See the poem fragment "The Pious Man Speaks," in Nietzsche (1993A).

31 See *Les mots et les choses* (1966). Also, the interview "L'homme est-il mort?" reprinted as Foucault (1994C).

32 These issues are themselves generally underestimated. The current popularity of the word "dis-course" in all manner of fairly conventional social science is the best indication of this. Anyone who uses this word with a nod to Foucault but would repudiate the following claim is one such underestimator: in matters of social and cultural analysis, there is nothing outside discourse. The qualifier "in matters of..." aims at both the *contextuality* of the claim and the existence of a limit against which social matters come up, a *limit* that cannot be named, and that can be approached by pointing to the experience of death.

a pronoun in the English language, and that in using it you are designating yourself. Knowledge of this linguistic resource, the first-person pronoun, allows the speaker to position her/himself in a situation. But once we start questioning the fact of your utterance "I am going out," we find that the position you indicated as yours is derived from the variety of pronouns available, among which one is chosen as appropriate. Thus, language comes first, and subjects second. This relationship between language and the subject has been one of the great themes of art and philosophy since at least the late nineteenth century. Think for instance of Baudelaire's famous line "Je est un autre" (I is another).

How are infinity and the limit implicated in this relationship between language and subject? First, on infinity, which will eventually lead us to the limit: as Gary Gutting writes in his explication of Foucault's work until 1971, once discourse is foregrounded, "language cannot be entirely reduced to an object, since it always reappears in the subject's effort to express what he knows" (Gutting, 1989: 195). Foucault's own version of this is best expressed in "La pensée du dehors" (1994B [1966]), a reflection on the work of writer Maurice Blanchot. Foucault writes that "the being of language only appears for itself in the disappearance of the subject" (1994B: 520-1; my translation[33]). Once we start looking at the "I" in the sentence "I am going out," we concern ourselves with the language available to you, the speaker; and your self-identification as "I" is seen to be derived from the possibilities afforded by the language. "Thought from outside" is that which "stands outside any and all subjectivity, the limits of which it exposes as though from outside, stating its end, making its dispersion scintillate, gathering only its invincible absence..." (Foucault, 1994B: 521; my translation[34]). As, clearly, no writer or artist can stand "outside all subjectivity" (something that Foucault obviously recognizes), the point / goal is to approach the limit of subjectivity. We are close, here, to the a/individualism of the mystic's experience, and to the impossibility of communicating such experience through language.

The same theoretical structure underlies Foucault's reluctance at claiming a positive political project. Given the impossibility of getting out, outright, of the prisonhouse[35] of language, and power being immanent to human relations, how can one propose (in discourse) alternatives as positive goods involving liberation? It cannot be done. One may resist, however. And, through art and literature for instance, one may glimpse the edge

---

33 The original French text is: "l'être du langage n'apparaît pour lui-même que dans la disparition du sujet."

34 (La pensée du dehors, c'est) "(c)ette pensée qui se tient hors de toute subjectivité pour en faire surgir comme de l'extérieur les limites, en énoncer la fin, en faire scintiller la dispersion et n'en recueillir que l'invincible absence..."

35 James W. Bernauer writes that "(t)he single experience that was always at the source of (Foucault's) thought was the reality of imprisonment, the incarceration of human beings within modern systems of thought and practice which had become so intimately a part of them that they no longer experienced these systems as a series of confinements but embraced them as the very structure of being human" (Bernauer, 1987: 45).

(again, not of the cliff, but of the razor). This is *approaching*[36] the limit-experience. As the edge of language is glimpsed, it is also subjectivity and "Man" that are brought to their limit – they are, to say the least, decentred, calling "the outside" into notional view (that is to say, we can infer that there is such a space as the outside). And, given its conceptual relationship to our ordinary discursive worlds, it seems quite appropriate to situate this "outside" within the broad reaches of spirituality. Which brings me, briefly, to the second (seeming) paradox: affirming an autonomous spiritual space, after having shied away from positive political projects and having decried the tyranny of grand narratives.

Foucault further writes of "thought from outside" that it is discourse, "even though it is beyond all language, silence, beyond all being, nothingness" (1994B: 521; my translation[37]). Thus, we have a discourse that is a void, a silence: hardly a grand narrative.

A good parallel to Foucault's presentation of *la pensée du dehors* can be found in the dialogue between Zen patriarch Ma-tsu Tao-i and a disciple:

> Once a disciple asked him, "Why does Your Reverence say that this very mind is Buddha?" "In order to stop the crying of little children," Ma-tsu replied. The disciple asked further, "When the crying has stopped, what then?" Ma-tsu said, "Then I would say that this very mind which is Buddha is in reality neither mind nor Buddha." (Wu, 1996: 72)

If such teaching can be said to be a fragment of a grand narrative, it is one that works constantly at undermining its own propositions; as a narrative, it collapses upon itself, indifferent, or indeed hostile, to issues of truth. Rather than a grand narrative, then, one might suggest that Zen Buddhism is in fact an anti-narrative. The same could be said of the spirituality enacted in the elders' saying quoted at the beginning of this chapter: "Everybody has a song to sing which is no song at all: it is a process of singing, and when you sing, you are where you are." There is something here that is very much attuned to experiencing the limit, and very much like what Foucault identifies as "thought from outside."

> Cease to listen with the ear, but listen with the mind.
> Cease to listen with the mind, but listen with the spirit.
> The function of the ear is limited to hearing; the function
> of the mind is limited to forming images and ideas. As to
> the spirit, it is an emptiness responsive to all things.
> – CONFUCIUS, in an imaginary conversation[38]

---

36 Approaching: a key concept in the philosophy of Gaston Bachelard, a significant influence on Foucault's worldview. See Gutting (1989).

37 (La pensée du dehors est) "(d)iscours donc, même si elle est, au-delà de tout langage, silence, au-delà de tout être, néant."

38 In Wu (1996: 27).

Conclusion

Expect aurora borealis

←————————————————————————————————→

Materially, for us in the West and for every human society, individual autonomy is limited. It always exists in the context of family and community, however these might be defined. Is it inherently a conservative thing to write this? I would think that it is so far from being conservative that it just might be a condition for expanding democracy (see Mouffe, 1994). Here is, in a few concluding words, why.

If we look at what is involved in being conservative, we find among other things that "obligations always take precedence over rights" (Giddens, 1994: 25). More generally, the self-described conservative Roger Scruton writes that "(t)he conservative places his faith in arrangements that are known and tried, and wishes to imbue them with all the authority necessary to constitute an accepted and objective public realm" (quoted in Giddens, 1994: 28).

I would venture to say that poststructuralists (and others often disparaged as relativists) would more often than not place themselves on the left, rather than the right of the political spectrum.[1] Theoretically, we would seek to undermine the rights/obligations couple as an either/or dichotomy, at the same time that we would ask what power relations are taken up in this couple; politically, we would certainly not want to bolster the obligations side at the expense of the rights side. On Scruton's definition, it is liberals who appear conservative. By sounding as though liberalism is synonymous with virtue and civilization and thereby implying that non-liberals are somehow barbarous, they suggest a democratic obligation to be liberal, overriding the freedom to argue that other positions are also civilized. Furthermore, their

---

1   In fact, in North America much of the impetus for work variously described as postmodern or poststructuralist is directly connected to left-wing politics, and more specifically to the difficulties encountered by (neo-)Marxism in the late 1970s and the 1980s. See for instance Nicholson and Seidman (1995).

strenuous defense of the known arrangements of liberal democracy, aiming to bolster those arrangements' authority, is in sharp contrast to poststructuralist exertions to undermine the legitimacy of various power arrangements of whitestream modernity.

Judith Shklar's (1989) liberalism of fear feeds upon the inheritance of Europe's violent and oppressive past, and on "the most ancient of Indo-European traditions... the caste society" which, by putting individuals into pre-determined boxes, is not respectful of individual autonomy: given the alternatives, she says, we ought to favour liberalism. But we should get out of Europe. We should, that is, see the European experience for what it is: a regional experience, with no God-given privilege to speak for all humanity, and certainly no special wisdom inaccessible to other regions. Once we recognize this, the next step is to look elsewhere for lessons in political and moral philosophy.

It is perhaps clear that when a caste system includes severe inequalities (such as in the recent history of India), there is not much to recommend it. But is it the caste system in itself that is the problem, or should one focus on the inequalities? For while liberal societies do not have official castes, a homeless person in Canada cannot be much better off than a low-caste person. And if extreme poverty has receded in much of the West, it is not clear that this has to do with liberalism *per se* – besides, great poverty looks as if it might be making a comeback in the context of globalizing neo-liberalism. As well, while it is clear that a caste system restricts individual choice, the alternative of a liberalism-carrying class system is not one of absolute freedom of choice: social mobility exists but is limited, and a whole variety of factors beyond individual preference intervene in a person's educational and career path. As a result, it is not rare in Western societies for individuals to be unhappy with their "place".

This is (obviously) not to promote caste systems or other forms of restrictions on individual choice, but rather to point out that the material differences in individual autonomy between today's West and other societies are not as great as liberal ideology would suggest. In any case, they are not differences of kind, but of degree. And there are societies where inequalities were / are lesser than what is found in the West.

Liberal ideology is, in some sense, the West at its best – the West as it likes to dream itself. In another sense, liberalism is the West at its worst in that this dream is constituted by a derogatory comparison with other forms of life: they were (or are) cruel and we are better than that; they were (or are) contemptuous of individual autonomy, which we value most. But liberal ideology is not, by any means, an accurate description of life anywhere on this planet. Indeed, there is something strange in this dream of a society that would put no constraints whatsoever upon individuals. It is the fantasy of the end of society itself, a dream of unanimity and the end of conflict that, in its "aversion for reality", may be a danger to democracy (Mouffe, 1994: 164, quoting Stuart Hampshire). In fact, such a fantasy is perhaps a necessary component of a worldview that casts out spirituality and replaces it with politics. It is the ghost of the spirit, lingering within modernity.

● ● ●

With specific regard to a case such as *Peters v. Campbell*, the urge to undermine established arrangements calls for taking liberal modernity off its pedestal. This is necessary if we are to stop looking down on other traditions, if we are to start learning from them – if we are to be able to get out of Europe. The late Judith Shklar might have said that such an argument smacks of "absolute relativism", which is

> too complacent and too ready to forget the horrors of our world to be credible. It is deeply illiberal, not only in its submission to tradition as an ideal, but in its dogmatic identification of every local practice with deeply shared local human aspirations. (Shklar, 1989: 34)

I am not sure that many scholars who get tarred with the brush of "absolute relativism" would recognize either the label or this description as fitting their own practice. I certainly do not. Let us look at the specific claims and their fit to my analysis of the initiation of Joseph Peters; then, we will go back to the label. Three claims deserve particular attention: first, that of forgetfulness of our world's horrors; second, that tradition as such is set up as an ideal; third, that every single local practice is to be honoured.

First, it is precisely the horror that our whitestream modern world has visited upon indigenous peoples of the Americas[2] that requires a re-evaluation of our relationship with them. Illiberal states (Brazil, Argentina, Guatemala, to name but a few) and liberal democratic states (Canada, the US) alike, taking whitestream superiority for granted, have endeavoured to eliminate "primitive" cultures by extermination, assimilation, or both. The process is still on-going today. Indeed, it is significant that, when writing of the United States, Shklar (1989) only pointed to the oppression of African-Americans as undermining the country's liberalism; aboriginal peoples in the United States are just invisible.

In Canada, as recently as 1969, it was precisely in the name of liberalism that the federal government unveiled the incredibly named *White Paper on Indian Policy*, which sought "the removal of Indian special status and the remaking of Indians into 'Canadians as all other Canadians'" (Boldt, 1993; see also Frideres, 1988). This new, thoroughly liberal and modern policy was

---

2   As well as various parts of Australasia.

shelved only in the face of overwhelming First Nations' opposition. There is nothing complacent in taking a hard look at what we have done and continue doing to other peoples, in the name of a universality to which we have no more right than they do.

Second, it is not a submissiveness toward tradition that leads one to the kind of analysis I have been presenting here. Tradition as such, theirs or ours, is of no interest. It is the living, current practice of individuals and groups that is of primary importance along with the respect one ought to have for others and their practices, unless and until solid reasons have been provided for denying that respect. Tradition becomes relevant when one considers that all practices, of all peoples (including us moderns), are culturally, traditionally embedded. Someone may claim the authority of tradition to legitimize (or decry) a current practice, but my evaluation of that practice need not be impressed by that authority. Thus, female genital mutilation may rest on long-standing tradition, but I am no more inclined to defer to it than if it had been instituted yesterday. The same logic applies, I am afraid, to liberal tradition, the authority of which is invoked rashly to condemn the current practice of syewen.

We are already dealing, at this point, with Shklar's third claim, about the presumed relativist worship of "every local practice." It is by looking closely and with an open mind at a specific practice, such as syewen, that an outsider may make some sense of it and distinguish it (or not) from other practices in one's own and other cultures. Only then can one answer a question such as "does syewen belong in the same category as genital mutilation?". And only then can an outsider hope to be in a position to make an informed moral and political judgement about that specific practice. There is no blanket worship of local practices – theirs or ours – in this attitude. On the contrary: it starts from recognizing that our own whitestream practices are themselves local, that therefore they provide no objective standards for assessing other localities, and that moral and political deliberation is all the more necessary because it sits on unstable, relative ground.

● ● ●

The claim that relativists dogmatically identify with every local practice is not only inaccurate, it is nonsensical. By arguing for the legitimacy of syewen, for example, I am condemning the (local) whitestream practice of looking down on aboriginal cultures as savage or barbarous. Identifying with both is impossible: stepping back from them both and saying that they are both legitimate because they are both local would not do the job, for this would be to identify with "the local" as a universal category, and not with the practices themselves. If there are "absolute relativists" who do this (and I doubt that this is the case), they are contradicting themselves. This means that relativists must choose between local practices, those with which we will identify, and others of which we will take a dim view. It is because we sometimes (or often) side with practices outside the whitestream that liberals and other universalists get so exercised about relativism. This is offensive to someone like Shklar, because she seems unable to imagine anything outside the facile opposition between liberalism and "political tyranny." Thus, her sense of other forms of social order is absurdly caricatural:

> The unspoken and sanctified practices that prevail within every tribal border can never be openly analyzed or appraised, for they are by definition already permanently settled within the communal consciousness. Unless there is an open and public review of all the practical alternatives, especially of the new and alien, there can be no responsible choices and no way of controlling the authorities that claim to be the voice of the people and its spirit. (Shklar, 1989: 34)

I will not even comment on the blanket disparagement contained in the phrase "every tribal border."[3] Let us just look at the Coast Salish situation as a counter-example, which will take care of the universal application of Shklar's statement. In cultures such as the Coast Salish, "sanctified practices" are very much spoken. This is such a fundamental characteristic of societies centred on an oral tradition that it seems almost silly to have to point it out. The oral tradition indeed ensures that cultural norms are "open and public" in a way much more profound than what Europeans have developed. And so when alternatives present themselves – Christianity's arrival in the Americas, for example – they are examined and compared with the extant order. Nothing, consequently, is "permanently settled." There is, rather, a non-stop dialogical process and negotiation between "authorities" and the people, leading to dynamic historical transformation. What can it mean, then, to claim that liberal governance is the only way to produce "responsible choices"? It would be hard to comprehend, in fact, that such a nightmarish fantasy of the "tribal" would remain current in liberal thought, if liberalism were not constituted by its difference with a degraded Other (see Chapter 3). Needless to say, this does not make the fantasy any more respectable.

For a relativist to identify, or side, with local practices outside his or her own cultural traditions, it is necessary to assume that at least some recognition is possible from one culture to another. What happens, then, to the standard poststructuralist (and otherwise postmodern) claim of incommensurability between descriptions of the world? First, its philosophical ambit

---

3 I do wonder whether a typographical error interfered with what should have read "every tribal order." But it makes no difference to the unthinking Euro-centrism of the claim.

becomes more clearly specified, while retaining its radicality. Second, it loses much of the polemical edge derived from its association with the issue of "cultural appropriation." And third, it removes a cognitive barrier to the consideration of actual contact and interaction between cultures in the historical process.

In my discussion of the initiation of Joseph Peters, I have tried to show, to illustrate, the possible recognition of one description of the world (let us call it 'A') by another ('B'), rather than to explain it. And this, I would claim, is the expression of the philosophical ambit of incommensurability. An explanation of this recognition would require one of two things. First, that description A serve as a standard by which description B is measured, or vice versa. But since we already know that A and B, the Coast Salish and whitestream descriptions of the world, are both local and independent from each other, making one the standard for the other would be unwarranted. The other possibility would be to find a third description, C, that would encompass A and B and serve as a standard for both – but such a C cannot exist, at least as a socially embedded language. Recognition, then, can be shown, pointed to, but it cannot be properly explained.

The philosophical point of this distinction between showing and explaining (or saying) is one of the few constants in Ludwig Wittgenstein's work, from his early *Tractatus Logico-Philosophicus* to his late, and posthumously published, *Philosophical Investigations*. Its importance for understanding the relationship between our two descriptions of the world is eloquently exemplified in Wittgenstein's thoughts on Sir James Frazer's *The Golden Bough*. This was a thirteen-volume opus described by Ray Monk, Wittgenstein's biographer, as a "monumental account of primitive ritual and magic" which Frazer tried to explain by situating them as an early step in the progress of science (Monk, 1991: 310).

Monk writes that Wittgenstein was not entirely impressed by Frazer's achievement: "The wealth of facts which Frazer had collected about these rituals would, Wittgenstein thought, be more instructive if they were presented without any kind of theoretical gloss and arranged in such a way that their relationships with each other – and with our own rituals – could be *shown*" (Monk, 1991: 311; emphasis in the original). A satisfactory alternative, Wittgenstein wrote, would be to arrange "the factual material so that we can easily pass from one part to another and have a clear view of it – showing it in a perspicuous way ... This perspicuous presentation makes possible that understanding which consists just in the fact that we 'see the connections'" (Wittgenstein, *Remarks on Frazer's Golden Bough*, quoted in Monk, 1991: 311).

We should see the connections; hence Wittgenstein's recommendation, "Don't think, but look!" Relationships within a system of rituals, and between systems of rituals, Wittgenstein writes, can be shown, can be pointed to, but cannot be explained.

On the political plane, this has two crucial consequences. First, the philosophical incommensurability radically disqualifies the Canadian judge in *Peters v. Campbell*; not so much because no judge could possibly "see the connections" in the circumstances surrounding the initiation of Joseph Peters, but because seeing the connections and acting on this basis would be acting as someone other than a Canadian judge. For someone to be in a position to adjudicate the conflict between Joseph Peters and his initiators on the basis of "seeing the connections," that someone would have to be within a system of aboriginal justice. Second, because relationships can be shown, because A and B can recognize something of themselves in each other, there is no obligation of silence about B on members of A's interpretive community, and vice versa. Members of each community are not incapable of knowing and understanding some of the other's terms; they may not be able to put themselves in the other's shoes, but they may be able to imagine what these shoes might be like. Looking at the other's shoes, it is possible to "see the connections." But this requires an openness to the other's ways and to dialogue which at once is the antithesis of "cultural authority" and makes "cultural appropriation" a non-issue.

One might also say that in the course of historical interaction between peoples, recognition between cultures happens every time that elements of one culture are integrated in the fabric of another by individuals and groups living in the meeting space. We have seen that, for instance, strong elements of Iroquois spirituality were brought into the Catholicism of converts at New France's Kanewake mission. We have also seen, conversely, that trance practices of the Shaker church have contributed to the revival of aboriginal practices among the Coast Salish people.

Social theory, and more specifically postcolonial social theory, must be able to make sense of such events, which testify among other things to the cultural dynamism of peoples living in oppressive conditions. To make sense of this, it is necessary to get past a blanket notion of incommensurability between cultures. An imbalance in social power, favouring the white stream, was integral to the conditions that produced the merging of previously foreign cultural elements. The fact remains that the merging happened, creating new cultural practices, in the Coast Salish case, practices strongly associated with aboriginality as a cultural and emancipatory project.

Should we conclude from this that *difference* loses its theoretic importance? Not exactly. What we see in the intercultural recognition portrayed here is not the kind of "unbiased communication" (as Habermas would say) that could found a renewed universalism. Communication between the two cultures is not easy; their codes are far from transparent to each other, and the power imbalances are enormous. Thus, there is a large gap between a belief in absolute incommensurability and a renewed universalism.

Critics of postmodern perspectives try to discredit them by setting up the alternatives of going forward with the promise of Enlightenment or of turning one's back on it — the latter alternative being supposedly postmodern, and of course entirely disreputable. Such critics will not entertain the possibility of taking the Enlightenment sideways, as it were or, as Oliver Wendell Holmes suggested, of rejecting both horns of the dilemma by moving to another plane. Somewhere in between the stark opposition between bright light and pitch dark, between easy intercultural translation and stone silence, the initiation of Joseph Peters tells me that difficult communication, weak communication is possible based on the possibility of recognition, of "seeing the connections." And that in between a belief in infinite progress through politics and a despairing political quietism in the face of social ills, there is room for a limited, difficult, weak politics.

I am borrowing this notion of weakness somewhat freely from the "philosophy of weak thought," an Italian version of poststructuralism where: "The use of the adjective 'weak' refers to the necessity for 'reason' to operate within a dimension of light and shade..." (Borradori, 1987-88: 40). It is in this spirit that I read Seamus Heany's poem "North":

> Compose in darkness.
> Expect aurora borealis
> in the long foray
> but no cascade of light.[4]

There are several layers of philosophical considerations entailed by this stance, which I will have to leave aside, so as to focus my last comments on a question of politics: does this possibility of recognition between cultures undermine the aboriginal claim to a right to self-government? The short answer is: no.

The first thing to remember is that my "attempt to think differently," while aiming at approaching an aboriginal perspective, remained firmly anchored within an occidental description of the world. I may be able, within my own language, to make some sense of aboriginal ways, but once I have redescribed some of their cultural language into my own, I have not produced one single language, one single description of the world. It is as when I began: there are two cultures, two descriptions of the world. Not one. To claim otherwise would be to reinstate the exact cultural authority which I have tried to destabilize.

Second, the key word in the claim to self-government remains *inherent*, which refers not to difference so much as to historical precedence.

4 Seamus Heany, "North" (1975), reproduced in *Selected Poems 1966-1987* (New York: The Noonday Press, Farrar, Straus and Giroux, 1991): 69-70.

Aboriginal peoples were here first, with their own (various) ways to govern themselves, and they never gave that up. This alone is sufficient for aboriginal peoples to be entitled, on their own terms, to self-government. Once they achieve self-government, they could very well decide to adopt the exact same institutions as whitestream Canada, but separately. The fact that they are not likely to do it speaks of an enduring and profound difference.

Third, approaching aboriginal culture as I have tried to do here results in building trust toward the other culture. For non-aboriginals who, like me, value freedom, equality, and democratic rights, there is something seriously unsettling about reading *The Globe and Mail*'s account of the initiation of Joseph Peters. Here is an apparently arbitrary "grabbing" of a man against his will, followed by a ritual that appears to involve injuries, starvation, and humiliations, and that is claimed to be part of collective aboriginal rights.

This newspaper story put me in a situation where I had to swallow hard and compromise one of two important principles. Now, I can see that the initiation of Joseph Peters was quite possibly justified under my own description of the world. This, by the way, does not mean that I endorse to any great extent the ways in which "my" society deals with "deviance." But I am modern, liberal even, and "of my society," at least to the extent that I find it difficult to accept the infliction of injuries and the override of consent under any circumstances. When I began working on the project that led to this book, I strongly supported the aboriginal claim to an inherent right to self-government, but not without some misgivings. I can now support it with a lighter heart, if few illusions.

Bibliography

◄───►

Ammerman, Nancy. 1994. "Telling Congregational Stories." *Religious Research*. 35:4 (June).

Amoss, Pamela. 1978. *Coast Salish Spirit Dancing: The Survival of an Ancient Religion*. Seattle and London: University of Washington Press.

Anderson, Benedict. 1991. *Imagined Communities. Reflections on the Origin and Spread of Nationalism*. 2nd edition. London & New York: Verso.

Asch, Michael. 1992. "Errors in Delgamuukw: An Anthropological Perspective," in *Aboriginal Title in British Columbia: Delgamuukw v. The Queen*. Edited by Frank Cassidy. Lantzville (BC) and Montreal: Oolichan Books and The Institute for Research on Public Policy: 221-243.

————. Forthcoming. "From Calder to Van der Peet: Aboriginal Rights and Canadian Law," in *New Frontiers: Constitutionalizing Aboriginal Rights in Australia, Canada and New Zealand*. Edited by P. Havemann. Oxford: Oxford University Press.

Ashcroft, Bill & Gareth Griffiths, Helen Tiffin, eds. 1995. *The Post-colonial Studies Reader*. London and New York: Routledge.

Bakan, Joel. 1991. "Constitutional Interpretation and Social Change: You can't always get what you want (nor what you need)," *Canadian Bar Review*. 70: 307-328.

Bastide, Roger. 1972. *Le rêve, la transe et la folie*. Paris: Flammarion.

————. 1975. *Le sacré sauvage*. Paris: Payot.

Bataille, Georges. 1986 [1957]. *Erotism: Death and Sensuality*. San Francisco: City Lights Books.

————. 1989 [1961]. *The Tears of Eros*. San Francisco: City Lights Books.

Bernauer, James W. 1987. "Michel Foucault's ecstatic thinking," in *The Final Foucault*. Edited by James W. Bernauer and David Rasmussen. Cambridge (Mass.): The MIT Press / Philosophy and Social Criticism: 45-82.

Berry, Philippa & Andrew Wernick, eds. 1992. *Shadow of Spirit. Postmodernism and Religion*. London and New York: Routledge.

Best, Steven. 1995. *The Politics of Historical Vision: Marx, Foucault, Habermas*. New York: The Guilford Press.

Bibby, Reginald W. 1990. *Mosaic Madness: The Poverty and Potential of Life in Canada*. Toronto: Stoddard.

Borradori, Giovanna. 1987-88. "'Weak Thought' and Postmodernism: The Italian Departure from Deconstruction," *Social Text*. 18 (Winter): 39-49.

Boldt, Menno. 1993. *Surviving as Indians: The Challenge of Self-Government*. Toronto: University of Toronto Press.

Brown, Craig, ed. 1987. *The Illustrated History of Canada*. Toronto: Lester & Orpen Dennys.

Budick, Sanford & Wolfgang Iser, eds. 1987. *Languages of the Unsayable. The Play of Negativity in Literature and Literary Theory*. Stanford (Cal.): Stanford University Press.

Burrows, John. 1997 (forthcoming). "Contemporary Traditional Equality: The Effect of the Charter on First Nations Politics," in *Charting the Consequences: The Impact of the Charter Rights on Law and Politics in Canada*. Edited by D. Schneiderman & K. Sutherland. Toronto: University of Toronto Press.

Butler, Judith & Joan W. Scott, eds. 1992. *Feminists Theorize the Political*. New York and London: Routledge.

Canada, Royal Commission on Aboriginal Peoples. 1996A. *Report of the Royal Commission on Aboriginal Peoples Volume 1: Looking Forward, Looking Back*. Ottawa: Minister of Supplies and Services Canada.

————, Royal Commission on Aboriginal Peoples. 1996B. *Report of the Royal Commission on Aboriginal Peoples. Volume 2: Restructuring the Relationship, part one*. Ottawa: Minister of Supplies and Services Canada.

Cardin, Jean-François. 1990. *Comprendre Octobre 1970: Le FLQ, la Crise et le syndicalisme*. Montreal: Méridien.

———— & Claude Couture, Gratien Allaire. 1996. *Histoire du Canada: Espace et différences*. Québec: Presses de l'Université Laval.

Carrigan, D. Owen. 1991. *Crime and Punishment in Canada: A History*. Toronto: McClelland & Stewart.

Carter, Sarah. 1990. *Lost Harvests: Prairie Indian Reserve Farmers and Government Policy.* Montreal & Kingston: McGill-Queen's University Press.

Cassidy, Frank, ed. 1992. *Aboriginal Title in British Columbia: Delgamuukw v. The Queen.* Lantzville (BC) & Montreal: Oolichan Books & The Institute for Research on Public Policy.

Cavell, Stanley. 1994. *A Pitch of Philosophy.* Cambridge (Mass.): Harvard University Press.

Cohen, Andrew. 1990. *A Deal Undone: The Making and Breaking of the Meech Lake Accord.* Vancouver: Douglas & McIntyre.

Commissioners' Report. 1992. *First Nations Circle on the Constitution: To the Source.* Ottawa: Assembly of First Nations (13 April).

Cornell, Drucilla. 1992. *The Philosophy of the Limit.* New York and London: Routledge.

Couture, Joseph. 1991. "Explorations in Native Knowing," in *The Cultural Maze. Complex Questions on Native Destiny in Western Canada.* Edited by J. W. Friesen. Calgary: Detselig Enterprises: 53-73.

Cox, Harvey. 1995. "The Warring Visions of the Religious Right," *The Atlantic Monthly,* November: 59-69.

Crosby, Christina. 1992. "Dealing with Differences," in *Feminists Theorize the Political.* Edited by J. Butler & J.W. Scott. New York & London: Routledge: 130-143.

Crow, Joan. 1992. "Standing on Principle: The Constitution and First Nations," *Kinesis,* April: 7, 8.

Cumming, Carman and Catherine McKercher. 1994. *The Canadian Reporter: News Writing and Reporting.* Toronto: Harcourt Brace Canada.

de Certeau, Michel. 1987 (1982). *La fable mystique, 1.* xvie-xviie siècle, 2nd edition. Paris: Gallimard, Coll. Tel.

Demos, John. 1995. *The Unredeemed Captive. A Family Story From Early America.* New York: Alfred A. Knopf.

Denis, Claude. 1989. "The Genesis of American Capitalism: An Historical Enquiry into State Theory," *The Journal of Historical Sociology* 2:4 (December): 328-56.

———. 1995. "'Government can do whatever it wants': Moral regulation in Ralph Klein's Alberta", *The Canadian Review of Sociology and Anthropology* 32:3 (August): 365-383.

Denis, Claude. 1996. "Sovereignty Postponed: On the Canadian way of losing a referendum, and then another," *Constitutional Forum*, Fall 1995 – Winter 1996: 44-51.

Derrida, Jacques. 1987A. *De l'esprit. Heidegger et la question*. Paris: Galilée.

————. 1987B. "How to avoid speaking: Denials," in *Languages of the Unsayable: The Play of Negativity in Literature and Literary Theory*. Edited by S. Budick & W. Iser. Stanford (Cal.): Stanford University Press: 3-70.

Desbarats, Peter. 1990. *Guide to Canadian News Media*. Toronto: Harcourt Brace Jovanovich, Canada.

Despland, Michel. 1988. "Henri Alline (1748-1784)," in *Folie, mystique et poésie*. Edited by Raymond Lemieux. Quebec: GIFRIC, Coll. Noeud: 113-120.

Diamond, Sara. 1995. *Roads to Dominion: Right-Wing Movements and Political Power in the United States*. New York: The Guilford Press.

Donoghue, Denis. 1996. "The Philosopher of Selfless Love," *The New York Review of Books*. XLIII: 5 (March 21): 37-40.

Dumm, Thomas L. 1996. *Michel Foucault and the Politics of Freedom*. Thousand Oaks: Sage.

Dworkin, Ronald. 1996. "The Moral Reading of the Constitution," *The New York Review of Books*. XLIII: 5 (21 March): 46-50.

Easton, Susan M. 1983. *Humanist Marxism and Wittgensteinian Social Philosophy*. Manchester: Manchester University Press.

Eisenstein, Zillah R. 1994. *The Color of Gender. Reimaging Democracy*. Berkeley: University of California Press.

Eribon, Didier. 1990. *Michel Foucault*. Paris: Flammarion, Coll. Champs.

Ericson, Richard V. and Patricia M. Baranek, Janet B.L. Chan. 1991. *Representing Order: Crime, Law, and Justice in the News Media*. Toronto: University of Toronto Press.

Errington, Jane. 1993. "Pioneers and Suffragists," in *Changing Patterns. Women in Canada*. Edited by Sandra Burt, L. Code & L. Dorney. Toronto: McClelland & Stewart: 59-91.

Finley, M. I. 1983. *Politics in the Ancient World*. Cambridge: Cambridge University Press.

Fish, Stanley. 1989. *Doing What Comes Naturally. Change, Rhetoric, and the Practice of Theory in Literary and Legal Studies*. Durham & London: Duke University Press.

Fish, Stanley. 1995. *Professional Correctness: Literary Studies and Political Change.* Oxford & New York: Oxford University Press.

Fitzpatrick, Peter. 1992. *The Mythology of Modern Law.* London & New York: Routledge, Sociology of Law and Crime Series.

Fogelin, Robert J. 1996. "Wittgenstein's critique of philosophy," in *The Cambridge Companion to Wittgenstein.* Edited by H. Sluga & D.G. Stern. Cambridge: Cambridge University Press: 34-58.

Foucault, Michel. 1971. *L'ordre du discours.* Paris: Gallimard.

————. 1972 [1961]. *Histoire de la folie à l'âge classique.* Paris: Gallimard.

————. 1975. *Surveiller et punir: Naissance de la prison.* Paris: Gallimard.

————. 1976. *La volonté de savoir: Histoire de la sexualité*, volume 1. Paris: Gallimard.

————. 1984A. *L'usage des plaisirs. Histoire de la sexualité*, volume 2. Paris: Gallimard.

————. 1984B. *Le souci de soi. Histoire de la sexualité*, volume 3. Paris: Gallimard.

————. 1994A (1978). "Michel Foucault et le zen: un séjour dans un temple zen," in *Dits et écrits, 1954-1988, Volume 3.* Edited by D. Defert & F. Ewald. Paris: Gallimard: 618-624.

————. 1994B (1966). "La pensée du dehors," in *Dits et écrits, 1954-1988, Volume 1.* Edited by D. Defert & F. Ewald. Paris: Gallimard: 518-539.

————. 1994C (1966). "L'homme est-il mort?" in *Dits et écrits, 1954-1988, Volume 1.* Edited by D. Defert & F. Ewald. Paris: Gallimard: 540-544.

————. 1994D (1961). "Préface à *Folie et déraison. Histoire de la folie à l'âge classique*," in *Dits et écrits, 1954-1988, Volume 1.* Edited by D. Defert & F. Ewald. Paris: Gallimard: 159-167.

————. 1994E (1972). "Les intellectuels et le pouvoir," in *Dits et écrits, 1954-1988, Volume 2.* Edited by D. Defert & F. Ewald. Paris: Gallimard: 306-315.

Fournier, Pierre. 1990. *Autopsie du Lac Meech.* Montreal: VLB Éditeur.

Francis, Daniel. 1992. *The Imaginary Indian: The Image of the Indian in Canadian Culture.* Vancouver: Arsenal Pulp Press.

Fraser, Nancy. 1989. *Unruly Practices: Power, Discourse and Gender in Contemporary Social Theory.* Minneapolis: University of Minnesota Press.

Frideres, James. 1988. *Native Peoples in Canada: Contemporary Conflicts.* Scarborough (On.): Prentice-Hall Canada.

Gawthrop, Daniel. 1996. *High-Wire Act: Power, Pragmatism, and the Harcourt Legacy.* Vancouver: New Star Books.

Giddens, Anthony. 1984. *The Constitution of Society: Outline of the Theory of Structuration.* Cambridge: Polity Press.

————. 1994. *Beyond Left and Right. The Future of Radical Politics.* Stanford (Cal.): Stanford University Press.

Gómez-Moriana, Antonio & Danièle Trottier, eds. 1993. *L''indien', instance discursive.* Actes du Colloque de Montréal (1991). Candiac (Qc): les Éditions Balzac, Coll. L'Univers des discours.

Government of Canada. 1995. *Federal Policy Guide: Aboriginal Self-Government: The Government of Canada's Approach to Implementation of the Inherent Right and the Negotiation of Aboriginal Self-Government.* Ottawa: Minister of Public Works and Government Services Canada.

————, Province of British Columbia and Nisga'a Tribal Council. *Nisga'a Treaty Negotiations: Agreement-in-Principle*: 15 February, 1996.

Guédon, Marie Françoise. 1994. "Dene Ways and the Ethnographer's Culture," in *Being Changed by Cross-Cultural Encounters.* Edited by D. E. Young & J.G. Goulet. Peterborough (On.): Broadview Press: 39-70.

Gutting, Gary. 1989. *Michel Foucault's Archeology of Scientific Reason.* Cambridge: Cambridge University Press.

Guy, Donna J. 1992. "'White Slavery,' Citizenship and Nationality in Argentina," in *Nationalisms and Sexualities*, Edited by A. Parker et al. New York & London: Routledge: 201-217.

Habermas, Jürgen. 1975. *Legitimation Crisis.* Boston: Beacon Press.

————. 1987. *Lectures on the Philosophical Discourse of Modernity.* Cambridge (Mass.): The MIT Press.

Hill, Christopher. 1972. *The World Turned Upside Down: Radical Ideas during the English Revolution.* London: Temple Smith.

Hill-Tout, Charles. 1978. *The Salish People. The Local Contribution of Charles Hill-Tout, Volume IV: The Sechelt and the South-Eastern Tribes of Vancouver Island.* Edited with an Introduction by Ralph Maud. Vancouver: Talon Books.

Holmes, Stephen. 1989. "The permanent structure of antiliberal thought," in *Liberalism and the Moral Life.* Edited by N.L. Rosenblum. Cambridge (Mass): Harvard University Press.

Holmes, Stephen. 1993. *The Anatomy of Antiliberalism.* Cambridge (Mass.): Harvard University Press.

Hourani, Albert. 1991. *A History of the Arab Peoples*. Cambridge (Mass.): The Belknap Press of Harvard University Press .

Horowitz, Gad. 1992. "Groundless Democracy," in *Shadow of Spirit. Postmodernism and Religion*. Edited by P. Berry & A. Wernick. London & New York: Routledge: 156-164.

Hughes, Everett C. 1943. *French Canada in Transition*. Chicago: University of Chicago Press.

Ignatieff, Michael. 1993. *Blood and Belonging: Journeys into the New Nationalism*. Toronto: Viking.

Jeffries, Theresa M. 1993. "Sechelt Women and Self-Government," in *In Celebration of Our Survival*. Edited by D. Jensen & C. Brooks. Vancouver: UBC Press: 81-86.

Jensen, Doreen and Cheryl Brooks, eds. 1993 (1991). *In Celebration of Our Survival: The First Nations of British Columbia*. Vancouver: UBC Press.

Jilek, Wolfgang. 1974. *Salish Mental Health and Culture Change*. Toronto and Montreal: Holt, Rinehart and Winston.

Joffe, Josef. 1997. "Germany vs. The Scientologists," *The New York Review of Books*. 24 April: 16-21.

Joseph, Shirley. 1993. "Assimilation Tools: Then and Now," in *In Celebration of Our Survival*. Edited by D. Jensen & C. Brooks. Vancouver: UBC Press: 65-79.

Kent, Stephen A. 1987. "Puritan Radicalism and the New Religious Organizations: Seventeenth-Century England and Contemporary America," *Comparative Social Research*. 10: 3-46.

Krupat, Arnold. 1992. *Ethnocriticism: Ethnography, History, Literature*. Berkeley and Los Angeles: University of California Press.

Lamont, William. 1996. *Puritanism and Historical Controversy*. Montreal and Kingston: McGill-Queen's University Press.

Larue-Langlois, Jacques. 1989. *Manuel de Journalisme radio-télé*. Montreal: Éditions Saint-Martin.

Le Blanc, Benoît. 1988. "Où sont nos mystiques?" in *Folie, mystique et poésie*. Edited by Raymond Lemieux. Quebec City: GIFRIC, Collection Noeud: 65-70.

Lemieux, Raymond, ed. 1988A. *Folie, mystique et poésie*. Quebec City: GIFRIC, Collection Noeud.

———. 1988B. "Les mendiants de l'existence. Folie, mystique, poésie et ... science," in *Folie, mystique et poésie*. Edited by Raymond Lemieux. Quebec City: GIFRIC, Collection Noeud: 21-39.

Levinas, Emmanuel. 1989. "As if Consenting to Horror," *Critical Inquiry* (Winter).

Lind, Michael. 1995. "Rev. Robertson's grand international conspiracy theory," *The New York Review of Books*. 2 Feb.: 21-25.

Maier, Charles, ed. 1987. *Changing Boundaries of the Political*. Cambridge: Cambridge University Press.

Mandel, Michael. 1994. *The Charter of Rights and the Legalization of Politics in Canada*. Revised, updated and expanded edition. Toronto: Thompson Educational Publishing.

Mander, Jerry. 1991. *In the Absence of the Sacred: The Failure of Technology & the Survival of the Indian Nations*. San Francisco: Sierra Club Books.

Maracle, Lee. 1996. *I Am Woman: A Native Perspective on Sociology and Feminism*, 2nd edition. Vancouver: Press Gang Publisher.

Martel, Gilles. 1988. "Louis Riel, 8 décembre 1875. Les multiples expressions littéraires d'une expérience mystique," in *Folie, mystique et poésie*. Edited by Raymond Lemieux. Quebec: GIFRIC, Coll. Noeud: 141-146.

Marshall, Barbara L. 1994. *Engendering Modernity. Feminism, Social Theory and Social Change*. Boston: Northeastern University Press.

Marx, Karl. 1963. *Oeuvres choisies*, Vol. 1. Paris: Gallimard.

Mason Lee, Robert. 1996. "Reform Party's 'extremism' may be no more than a lack of sophistication," *The Globe and Mail*. March 16: D2.

Mercredi, Ovide & Mary Ellen Turpel. 1993. *In The Rapids: Navigating the Future of First Nations*. Toronto: Penguin Books.

Mettayer, Arthur. 1988. "Mère Marie de l'Incarnation ou toute la vie d'une mystique soutenue par les éléments structurants d'un de ses rêves," in *Folie, mystique et poésie*. Edited by Raymond Lemieux. Quebec City: GIFRIC, Collection Noeud: 99-111.

Milbank, John. 1992. "Problematizing the secular: the postmodern agenda," in *Shadow of Spirit. Postmodernism and Religion*. Edited by P. Berry and A. Wernick. London & New York: Routledge: 30-44.

Miller, James. 1993. *The Passion of Michel Foucault*. New York: Doubleday, Anchor Books.

Monière, Denis & Roch Côté, eds. 1995. *Québec 1996*. Montreal: Fides / *Le Devoir*.

Monk, Ray. 1991. *Ludwig Wittgenstein: The Duty of Genius*. London: Vintage.

Monture-Angus, Patricia A. 1996. "Lessons in Decolonization: Aboriginal Overrepresentation in Canadian Criminal Justice," in *Visions of the Heart: Canadian Aboriginal Issues*. Edited by D.A. Long & O.P. Dickason. Toronto: Harcourt, Brace Canada: 335-354.

Morris, Martin J. 1995. "Overcoming the Barricades: The Crisis at Oka as a Case Study in Political Communication," *The Journal of Canadian Studies*. 30:2 (Summer): 47-90.

Mouffe, Chantal. 1992. "Feminism, Citizenship and Radical Democratic Politics," in *Feminists Theorize the Political*. Edited by J. Butler & J.W. Scott. New York & London: Routledge: 369-384.

———. 1994. *The Return of the Political*. London & New York: Verso.

Narveson, Jan. 1993. *Moral Matters*. Peterborough: Broadview Press.

Nathan, Holly. 1993. "Native women demand end to justice project," *The Victoria Times-Colonist*. 11 January: A1, A2.

Nhât Hanh, Thích. 1995 (1973). *Zen Keys*. New York: Doubleday.

Nicholson, Linda and Steven Seidman, eds. 1995. *Social Postmodernism: Beyond Identity Politics*. Cambridge: Cambridge University Press.

Nietzsche, Friedrich. 1993A (1882-1887). *Le gai savoir*, in *Oeuvres* II. Translated by Henri Albert. Paris: Robert Laffont, Coll. Bouquins: 1-265.

———. 1993B (1886). *Par-delà le bien et le mal: Prélude à une philosophie de l'avenir*, in *Oeuvres* II. Translated by Henri Albert. Paris: Robert Laffont, Coll. Bouquins: 547-737.

O'Brien, Mary. 1981. *The Politics of Reproduction*. London: Routledge & Kegan Paul.

Olivier, Lawrence. 1995. *Michel Foucault: Penser au temps du nihilisme*. Montreal: Liber.

Owens, Craig. 1992. *Beyond Recognition: Representation, Power, and Culture*. Berkeley: University of California Press.

Parker, Andrew *et al.*, eds. 1992. *Nationalisms and Sexualities*. New York & London: Routledge.

Phillips, Anne. 1993. *Democracy and Difference*. University Park (Penn.): Pennsylvania State University Press.

Probyn, Elspeth. 1993. "True Voices and Real People: The 'Problem' of the Autobiographical in Cultural Studies," in *Relocating Cultural Studies. Developments in Theory and Research*. Edited by Valda Blundell *et al.* London & New York: Routledge.

Queen, Christopher S. & Sallie B. King. 1996. *Engaged Buddhism: Buddhist Liberation Movements in Asia*. Albany: State University of New York Press.

Rawls, John. 1972. *A Theory of Justice*. Oxford: Oxford University Press.

———. 1993. *Political Liberalism*. New York: Columbia University Press.

Rawlyk, G. A. 1984. *Ravished by the Spirit: Religious Revivals, Baptists, and Henry Alline*. Montreal & Kingston: McGill-Queen's University Press.

———. 1996. *Is Jesus Your Personal Saviour? In Search of Canadian Evangelicalism in the 1990s*. Montreal & Kingston: McGill-Queen's University Press.

Rorty, Richard. 1989. *Contingency, Irony, and Solidarity*. Cambridge: Cambridge University Press.

Rosenblum, Nancy L., ed. 1989. *Liberalism and the Moral Life*. Cambridge (Mass.): Harvard University Press.

Ross, Rupert. 1992. *Dancing with a Ghost: Exploring Indian Reality*. Markham (On.): Octopus Books.

———. 1996. *Returning to the Teachings: Exploring Aboriginal Justice*. Toronto: Penguin Books.

Said, Edward. 1978. *Orientalism*. New York: Random House.

———. 1981. *Covering Islam: How the Media and the Experts Determine How We See the Rest of the World*. New York: Pantheon Books.

Sayer, Derek. 1991. *Capitalism and Modernity. An excursus on Marx and Weber*. London & New York: Routledge.

Sewid-Smith, Daisy. 1993. "In Time Immemorial," in *In Celebration of Our Survival*. Edited by D. Jensen & C. Brooks. Vancouver: UBC Press: 16-32.

Shklar, Judith N. 1989. "The Liberalism of Fear," in *Liberalism and the Moral Life*. Edited by N.L. Rosenblum. Cambridge (Mass.): Harvard University Press: 21-38.

Silverman, Robert A. & M.O. Nielsen, eds. 1992. *Aboriginal Peoples and Canadian Criminal Justice*. Toronto & Vancouver: Butterworths.

Sioui, Georges. 1989. *Pour une autohistoire amérindienne*. Quebec City: Presses de l'Université Laval.

Smith, Melvin H. 1995. *Our Home or Native Land: What governments' aboriginal policy is doing to Canada*. Victoria: Crown Western.

Stone, Sharon D. 1993. "Getting the message out: Feminists, the press and violence against women," *The Canadian Review of Sociology and Anthropology* 30:3 (August): 377-400.

Suttles, Wayne. 1987. *Coast Salish Essays.* Vancouver & Seattle: Talon Books & University of Washington Press.

Taylor, Charles. 1985. *Human Agency and Language.* Cambridge: Cambridge University Press.

———. 1989. *Sources of the Self: The Making of the Modern Identity.* Cambridge (Mass.): Harvard University Press.

———. 1991. *The Malaise of Modernity.* Concord (On.): Anansi Press.

———. 1993. *Reconciling the Solitudes: Essays on Canadian Federalism and Nationalism.* Montreal & Kingston: McGill-Queen's University Press.

Taylor, J. 1994. "Pat Robertson's God, Inc." *Esquire.* November: 77-83.

Tester, Keith. 1994. *Media, Culture and Morality.* London & New York: Routledge.

Thompson E.P. 1993. *Witness Against the Beast: William Blake and the Moral Law.* New York: The New Press.

Todorov, Tzvetan. 1982. *La conquête de l'Amérique: La question de l'autre.* Paris: Seuil.

Touraine, Alain. 1992. *Critique de la modernité.* Paris: Fayard.

Tully, James. 1995. *Strange Multiplicity: Constitutionalism in an Age of Diversity.* Cambridge: Cambridge University Press.

Turner, Bryan S., ed. 1990A. *Theories of Modernity and Postmodernity.* London: Sage Publications.

———. 1990B. "Periodization and Politics in the Postmodern," *Theories of Modernity and Postmodernity.* Edited by B.S. Turner. London: Sage Publications: 1-13.

———. 1994. *Orientalism, Postmodernism & Globalism.* London & New York: Routledge.

Turpel, Mary Ellen. 1990. "Aboriginal Peoples and the Canadian Charter: Interpretive Monopolies, Cultural Differences," *Canadian Human Rights Yearbook 1989-1990.* Ottawa: University of Ottawa Human Rights Research and Education Centre: 3-45.

Voltaire. 1963 (1759). *Candide: A Bilingual Edition.* Translated and Edited by Peter Gay. New York: St Martin's Press.

Weatherford, Jack. 1991. *Native Roots: How the Indians Enriched America.* New York: Crown Publishers.

Weaver, Sally. 1993. "First Nations Women and Government Policy, 1970-92: Discrimination and Conflict," in *Changing Patterns: Women in Canada.* Edited by S. Burt, L. Code & L. Dorney. Toronto: McClelland & Stewart: 92-150.

Weedon, Chris. 1987. *Feminist Practice and Poststructuralist Theory.* Oxford & New York: Basil Blackwell.

Weir, Allison. 1996. *Sacrificial Logics: Feminist Theory and the Critique of Identity.* New York & London: Routledge, Thinking Gender Series.

Wernick, Andrew. 1992. "Post-Marx: theological themes in Baudrillard's America," in *Shadow of Spirit: Postmodernism and Religion.* Edited by P. Berry & A. Wernick. London & New York: Routledge: 57-71.

Williams, Patrick & Laura Chrisman, eds. 1994. *Colonial Discourse and Post-Colonial Theory: A Reader.* New York. Columbia University Press.

Williams Robert A. Jr. 1992. "Gendered Checks and Balances: Understanding the Legacy of White Patriarchy in an American Indian Cultural Context," *Georgia Law Review.* 24: 1019-1044.

Williams, Robert A. Jr. 1994. "Linking Arms Together: Multicultural Constitutionalism in a North American Indigenous Vision of Law and Peace," *California Law Review.* 82: 981-1049.

Williams, Rowan. 1992. "Hegel and the gods of modernity," in *Shadow of Spirit. Postmodernism and Religion.* Edited by P. Berry and A. Wernick. London & New York: Routledge: 72-80.

Wittgenstein, Ludwig. 1968 (1953). *Philosophical Investigations,* 3rd ed. London: Basil Blackwell.

Woehrling, José. 1993. *La Constitution canadienne et l'évolution des rapports entre le Québec et le Canada anglais, de 1867 à nos jours.* Edmonton: Centre d'études constitutionnelles, série Points de vue, no 4.

Woodcock, George. 1990. *British Columbia: A History of the Province.* Toronto. Douglas & McIntyre.

Wu, John C.H. 1996 (1967). *The Golden Age of Zen.* Introduction by Thomas Merton. New York: Doubleday.

York, Geoffrey and Lorraine Pindera. 1991. *People of the Pines: The Warriors and the Legacy of Oka.* Toronto: Little, Brown.

Young, David E. & J.G. Goulet, eds. *Being Changed by Cross-Cultural Encounters. The Anthropology of Extraordinary Experience.* Peterborough (On.): Broadview Press.

Young, Robert J.C. 1995. *Colonial Desire: Hybridity in Theory, Culture and Race.* London & New York: Routledge.

Zaehner R.C. 1994 (1960). *Hindu and Muslim Mysticism.* Oxford: Oneworld Publications / School of Oriental and African Studies.

Index

★　An asterix (★) indicates an alias.

DATE DUE